D1563087

Proust's Lesbianism

Proust's Lesbianism

Elisabeth Ladenson

Cornell University Press

Ithaca and London

First published 1999 by Cornell University Press

Printed in the United States of America

Cornell University Press strives to use environmentally responsible suppliers and materials to the fullest extent possible in the publishing of its books. Such materials include vegetable-based, low-VOC inks and acid-free papers that are recycled, totally chlorine-free, or partly composed of nonwood fibers. Books that bear the logo of the FSC (Forest Stewardship Council) use paper taken from forests that have been inspected and certified as meeting the highest standards for environmental and social responsibility. For further information, visit our website at www.cornellpress.cornell.edu.

Library of Congress Cataloging-in-Publication Data

Ladenson, Elisabeth.
    Proust's lesbianism / Elisabeth Ladenson.
      p. cm.
    Includes index.
    ISBN 0-8014-3595-1 (cloth : alk. paper)
    1. Proust, Marcel, 1871–1922. A la recherche du temps perdu.
  2. Proust, Marcel, 1871–1922—Characters—Lesbians. 3. Lesbians in literature.
  4. Homosexuality in literature. 5. Homosexuality and literature—France—History—19th century.   I. Title.
PQ2631.R63A82765 1999
843'912—dc21   98-38248

Cloth printing 10 9 8 7 6 5 4 3 2 1

for

B,

and for E:

sine quibus non hic liber

Contents

Acknowledgments

Although it was actually written during the summer of 1996 and the summer and fall of 1997, this project has been so long in the incubation that I feel it would be best to begin at the beginning. I owe, first of all, an immeasurable debt to my parents for instilling in me the intellectual curiosity to embark on this sort of career. In particular, I have inherited from my mother a love of literature—perhaps imprudently, she read all of Proust before I was born—and from my father an interest in all things unseemly, without which it would never have occurred to me to choose such a subject.

I want to thank Jean-Yves Pouilloux for renewing my jaded undergraduate interest in academic study, and for making me read Proust for the first time when I was supposed to be working on something else entirely. I also thank Frank Paul Bowman and Lucienne Frappier-Mazur for their help, encouragement, and high intellectual standards.

At Columbia University, my graduate study of Proust and Baudelaire and Proust and Mme de Sévigné led both directly and indirectly to the present work. The following people were extremely helpful to me during that time: Antoine Compagnon, Ann Douglas, Kathryn Gravdal, and, last but by no stretch of the imagination least, Michael Riffaterre, whose guidance, support, and encouragement have been crucially important to me over the years.

I am grateful for the intellectual and emotional support of numerous friends and colleagues. Rodica Diaconescu Blumenfeld and Mary Mc-Alpin helped me survive the early stages of Proustification. Jane Gallop has been a great source of inspiration to me since I first read *Thinking through the Body* as a graduate student. The following people deserve my heartfelt thanks for reading parts of the manuscript, offering invaluable commentary, and in some cases valiantly reading through multiple versions: Suzanne Cusick, Susan Fraiman, David Hult, Cheryl Krueger, Mary McKinley, and Elena Russo. I am also very grateful to Janet Beizer and Martha Noel Evans for their friendship and support. In addition, I thank Deborah Hamm and Susan Moss, who in their very different ways have helped keep me sane.

The Faculty of Arts and Sciences of the University of Virginia has accorded me several grants, including a Sesquicentennial Research Fellowship, which were instrumental in enabling me to complete this project. Special thanks are due former dean Raymond Nelson for his consistent support above and beyond the call of duty.

Chapter 1 owes its existence to Suzanne Nash, whose more than generous loan of a summer cottage in Presque Isle, Michigan, during the summer of 1996 allowed me to bang out the opening sections of the book in an idyllic setting, on a Remington portable typewriter purchased at the Alpena Salvation Army.

I am grateful to Leo Bersani for being kind enough to slog through an unfortunate early version of Chapter 2 and offer invaluable advice despite the fact that he really did not know me at all. I also want to thank Jim Creech for his thoughtful comments and encouragement, and A. James Arnold, who read Chapter 1 and tried to cure me of my taste for parentheses.

Finally, I owe much to the following people at Cornell University Press: Bernhard Kendler, for his perspicacious advice and sense of humor; Carol Betsch, for her patience, discernment, and charm; and Amanda Heller, for her prose-improving ministrations.

The pages that follow are lovingly dedicated to Brigitte Mahuzier and Emma Cobb, who read countless versions and kept me going throughout.

E. L.

A Note on the Text

All quotations from *À la recherche du temps perdu* are from Terence Kilmartin's three-volume revision of C. K. Scott Moncrieff's original translation, *Remembrance of Things Past* (New York: Random House, 1981), based on the first Bibliothèque de la Pléiade edition (Paris: Gallimard, 1954), edited by Pierre Clarac and André Ferré. Because the first Pléiade edition has since been superseded by a four-volume version, edited by Jean-Yves Tadié et al. (Paris: Gallimard, 1987–89), with a vast critical apparatus comprising many useful variants, I have included volume and page references to both the Moncrieff-Kilmartin and second Pléiade editions, the translation followed by the original. In cases where only one reference is given, I have cited only the French edition, as no equivalent exists in the translation. In a few instances I have altered translations slightly in order to preserve fidelity to the original text where the precise wording of the latter is important for my argument; such alterations are indicated in the notes.

Translations from other sources in French are my own unless otherwise noted.

Proust's Lesbianism

Introduction

Pussy Galore and the Daughters of Bilitis

For the past twenty years or so a movement has been afoot in the United States to reclaim, rediscover, and reinvent lesbian history. Overtly heterosexual works have been re-read for their lesbian subplots; numerous authors and other public figures of the distant and more recent past have been "outed" and their novels, poems, films, music, and letters reexamined in this light; and more or less openly lesbian or bisexual authors such as Gertrude Stein and Virginia Woolf have received renewed attention, no longer despite but specifically because of their sexuality.

This general outbreak of lesbian visibility has nevertheless left one aspect of the history of relations between women for the most part unexplored: the representation of female homoeroticism in male-authored texts. This relative neglect is not an oversight so much as the product of an ideological position. The project of uncovering a lesbian past is part of a larger movement that aims to restore a self-descriptive voice to marginalized groups which have traditionally been accounted for only from the standpoint of the normative center. For lesbian studies this has meant that, in general, representations of female homoeroticism in male-authored texts have been regarded as fraudulent, as a mythology to be debunked and superseded rather than examined.

This phenomenon hinges on what might be termed the Pussy Galore factor, after the memorably named, voluptuously butch lesbian in *Gold-*

finger, who finds herself unable, in the end, to resist the charms of James Bond. Pussy Galore, the arrogantly independent aviatrix who succumbs to the even more arrogantly phallic Bond, exemplifies the function of the lesbian as object of the male gaze. Common knowledge and popular culture tell us that straight men are turned on by the idea of women having sex with other women. (A corollary states that this is true especially, and perhaps only, if male absence is understood to be temporary or contingent.) One need only look at the success of the film *Basic Instinct,* peruse the average issue of *Penthouse,* or scan the "adult" section of any video store for confirmation of this maxim. Why it should be so is a question that has received scant attention, presumably because the appeal of Pussy Galore seems fundamentally offensive in the epistemological context that would seem most apt for its study, and fundamentally self-evident in any other. But the fact is that it is extremely difficult to construct a lesbian past without taking into account male fantasies of lesbianism.

A salient case in point: the first lesbian organization in the United States was the Daughters of Bilitis, founded in the mid-1950s and enduring into the 1970s. Daughters of Bilitis, originally conceived as a social network to give middle-class women an alternative to lesbian bars, became an important political force as well and published a magazine, *The Ladder,* from 1956 to 1972.

What makes Daughters of Bilitis especially interesting, to my mind, is its name. The organization adopted this name, and not something more recognizable, such as Daughters of Sappho or Daughters of Gertrude Stein, so as to ensure the discretion that was its necessary watchword. Still, it is remarkable that the first lesbian organization in the United States took its name from the decadent semipornographic work of a French male author. Pierre Louÿs's 1894 *Chansons de Bilitis* consists of a series of prose poems that the author tried (successfully, at first) to pass off as his translation of a previously undiscovered Greek manuscript written by a pupil of Sappho. Despite its classical pretensions, Louÿs's work fits squarely into the tradition of *Goldfinger* and *Basic Instinct* and lesbian scenes in conventional pornography. Indeed, it is one of the texts that helped establish this tradition, of which nineteenth-century French literature is a cornerstone.

Lillian Faderman, one of the foremost historians of lesbianism in the United States, comes face to face with the conflict implied by the name

Daughters of Bilitis in her groundbreaking book *Surpassing the Love of Men* (1981), a history of "romantic friendship and love between women" in the West from the Renaissance to contemporary times. The book as a whole necessarily grapples with this problem: since it presents a narrative of progress from invisibility to self-affirmation, and since the most visible representations have been mainstream and male-authored, its trajectory must pass through the lesbian images in texts written by men.

In her third chapter, "Lesbian Exoticism," Faderman places *Chansons de Bilitis* in the context of works designed to appeal to male prurience, characterizing its vision of lesbianism as "promiscuous, fickle, narcissistic, sado-masochistic, and childishly based on a heterosexual model."[1] "Despite Louÿs's dedication of the poems 'to the young girls of the society of the future,'" she adds, "the poems are more apparently intended for the male reader" (274). Later in the book, in a chapter titled "The Rise of Lesbian-Feminism," Faderman discusses the founding of Daughters of Bilitis, and accounts for its name in a cagey parenthesis: "(named after Pierre Louÿs's song cycle, which had been dedicated to females of the future and appeared to be a relatively benign treatment of lesbianism)" (378).

What Faderman does not mention is that the founders of Daughters of Bilitis chose the name without realizing that Bilitis was the product of a prurient male literary imagination and not the genuine classical antecedant that they took her for. They were misled by Louÿs's prefatory "Life of Bilitis" with its elaborate historical verisimilitude that had earlier fooled a number of Hellenists.[2] The trivial if somewhat embarrassing fact that the founders of the country's first lesbian organization, in search of a classical heritage, inadvertently settled instead on a turn-of-the-century version of Pussy Galore suggests a larger problem as well: How is it possible to reclaim a true lesbian identity when even the celebratory images

---

1. Lillian Faderman, *Surpassing the Love of Men* (New York: Morrow, 1981), 274; subsequently cited in the text.

2. Del Martin and Phyllis Lyon, two of the founders of Daughters of Bilitis, tell the story of how the organization was named in their book *Lesbian/Woman* (San Francisco: Glide Publications, 1972), 219–20. On Louÿs's literary hoax itself, see Jean-Paul Goujon, *Pierre Louÿs: une vie secrète (1870–1925)* (Paris: Seghers, 1988), esp. 138–48.

of the past have been fashioned by and for men? In literature this tradition includes *Fanny Hill* and Swinburne in England and works by Baudelaire, Balzac, Gautier, and Louÿs in France. The much-discussed problem
of "lesbian invisibility" comes with a rider in the form of the all too visible tradition of pornographic and semipornographic representations of
women together. Especially in the wake of the recent upsurge in mainstream lesbian visibility, it is important to recognize the extent to which
lesbians still carry the legacy of "daughters of Bilitis" and to understand
that sometimes disquieting heritage.

In *Proust's Lesbianism* I address the question of how the already thorny issue of male representation of female homosexuality becomes further
complicated in the context of a work written by a gay man. The writings
of Marcel Proust occupy a prominent yet problematic place in the tradition to which I have alluded. The portrayal of lesbianism in *À la recherche
du temps perdu* is one of the most notorious and influential treatments of
the subject in modernist literature, indeed in all literature. Proust's conception of female homosexuality—"Gomorrah," as he calls it, as opposed
to "Sodom," or male homosexuality—both inherited the tradition of
Baudelaire's *Fleurs du mal,* Gautier's *Mademoiselle de Maupin,* Balzac's *Fille
aux yeux d'or,* and *Chansons de Bilitis,* and played an instrumental role in
forming the canon of lesbian images in literature as it developed over the
course of the twentieth century. His portrayal of female homosexuality
has been avidly read and commented on by such experts in the field as
Colette, Natalie Clifford Barney, Djuna Barnes, and, more recently,
Monique Wittig. No account of lesbianism in literature could be complete without coming to terms with Proust.

Meanwhile, just as histories of lesbianism try to ignore or dismiss male-
authored representations of it, Proust critics have tended to ignore or dismiss his representations of lesbianism. The view of sexual relations between women in the *Recherche* has been criticized and belittled by various
groups: by Proust critics, by those with a stake in the depiction of male
homosexuality, and also by readers specifically interested in the portrayal
of lesbianism in literature. Among the last, Proust has been accused of a
lack of verisimilitude, of having fabricated a depiction of lesbianism that
is actually a thinly disguised version of male homosexuality. Readers such

as Colette and Barney taxed Proust with not knowing what he was talking about when it came to relations between women.

Much the same accusation, albeit from a different point of view, has been leveled at Proust by readers less interested in the accuracy of his portrayal of lesbianism than in how he treated male homosexuality. André Gide in particular considered Proust a hypocrite for having imputed all the negative aspects of same-sex love to Sodom while cravenly reserving the positive aspects of romantic love for his "jeunes filles en fleurs."

Mainstream Proust critics, when they have considered the issue at all, have tended to make the same assumption about his lesbian characters: that they are "really" men. No matter what their other differences, readers over the decades have generally been in agreement on at least this one aspect of the *Recherche:* that the novel's account of female homosexuality must be read not as referring to relations between women but rather as a disguised expression of the author's own homosexuality.

Although Proust's "Gomorrah" fits squarely into an established tradition in French literature of representations of lesbianism in male-authored texts, the fact that its author was himself homosexual has led to a radically different interpretation from that accorded its predecessors. Despite its sapphic theme, for instance, *Chansons de Bilitis* was not scoured for suggestions of homosexuality on the part of its author so much as examined for evidence that he had made up the poems rather than translating them. Likewise, *Mademoiselle de Maupin* is rife with suggestions not only of lesbianism but of male homosexuality as well (albeit in the bet-hedging manner later exploited by the film and Broadway musical *Victor/Victoria,* in which a man briefly questions his sexuality because he finds himself attracted to a woman disguised as a man), and yet Gautier's sexual practices have not generally been an issue.

In the case of the *Recherche,* however, no other relation to lesbianism could be imagined on the part of a gay male author than that of displacement. By this I do not mean even the sort of displaced identification that may be read in the works of Mary Renault or Marguerite Yourcenar, in which a lesbian author explores issues of sexual identity through gay male characters. Instead, critics have most often seen in Proust's depiction of lesbianism a pure bait-and-switch trick whereby characters who are women in the text must instead be read as men.

I take a different approach to the problem of how to read Proust's Gomorrah. Instead of questioning what Gomorrah reveals about Sodom, I
have set out to understand what it means for a gay male author to have accorded such vast importance to his heterosexual male narrator's obsession
with lesbianism. It is only, I believe, by taking Proust's lesbian characters as
what he depicts them as being, rather than as necessarily standing for something else, that we can begin to grasp the place of femininity, and thus of
sexuality in general, in Proust's work. By the same token, an examination of
the way in which lesbianism is figured in male-authored texts has much to
tell us about constructions of masculinity and femininity in our culture.

I begin by providing an overview of the "transposition theory" of lesbianism in the *Recherche,* the idea that Gomorrah is a disguised version of
male homosexuality. After tracing the history of this reading, in Chapter
1, "Sexual/Textual Inversion," I analyze Proust's own somewhat incoherent framing of his depiction of female homosexuality as put forth publicly in his 1921 article "À propos de Baudelaire," and privately in his conversations with André Gide (recorded in the latter's *Journal*).

In the 1921 essay Proust posits two distinct kinds of relations between
male authors and their portrayals of lesbianism. On the one hand, he identifies the stance of the jealous lover whose mistress seeks consolation in the
arms of another women, a position Proust imputes to Alfred de Vigny,
whose poem "La Colère de Samson" he reads in the context of the poet's
affair with Marie Dorval, supposed lover of George Sand. To this heterosexual relation to lesbianism he opposes, on the other hand, the figure of
the complicitous male homosexual initiate in sapphic rituals, exemplified,
according to Proust's idiosyncratic reading, by Baudelaire in his "lesbian"
poems. The author implicitly situates his own position in alignment with
that of Vigny's heterosexual onlooker. He does so, I argue, in order to preclude the very reading of the role of lesbianism in the *Recherche* that his remarks on Baudelaire invite: that Gomorrah should be seen as a displaced
version of Sodom. The transposition-of-sexes hypothesis that has served
for decades to explain away the importance of Gomorrah in the novel is
thus at once sanctioned and denied by Proust himself.

In Chapter 2, "Gomorrah and Sodom," I examine Proust's depiction of
lesbianism in the *Recherche* with reference to the ways in which the implied symmetry between Sodom and Gomorrah breaks down. The analy-

sis is framed by a discussion of Colette's and Natalie Clifford Barney's remarks on Proust's Gomorrah; both take issue with what they perceive to be his insistence on the symmetry of male and female homosexualities, a symmetry that, I argue, is not borne out by the text itself. I analyze Proust's account of lesbianism in the context of late nineteenth-century sexology and early twentieth-century thought, arguing that Proust's own vocabulary of "inversion" fails to account for his portrayal of lesbianism. I also set the depiction of female sexuality in the novel against Freud's theories of sexual difference in order to show that Proust sees women as defined not by lack, as in Freud's view, but rather by a sort of self-sufficient plenitude. The sexual economy of the *Recherche,* I argue, is not based on a phallic model. Finally, I suggest that Gomorrah represents true "homosexuality," or attraction of sameness, as opposed to the essentially heterogendered notion of "inversion" in the novel. Like characters in Racinian tragedy, Proust's Sodomites are doomed to desire those who by definition cannot return their love, whereas his Gomorrheans present the novel's sole example of an erotic sensibility grounded in an aesthetics of sameness, and its only template of reciprocated desire.

In "Reading between the Blinds," the third chapter, I analyze various scenes of voyeurism in the *Recherche,* and deal with the question of the gaze and of voyeurism as epistemological penetration. Beginning with the Montjouvain scene—the novel's introduction to Gomorrah, in which the window shutters through which he is peeking are closed in the narrator's face at the crucial moment—I examine his energetic and always futile attempts to "see" female homosexuality. Proust paradoxically figures Gomorrah as at once exhibitionistic—female sexuality flaunting itself—and invisible, always eluding the male onlooker's efforts to apprehend, visually and conceptually, what women do together. Gomorrah, which flouts the stated laws of Proustian desire according to which love is concomitant with jealousy, acts as a willfully constructed epistemological blind spot, and it offers the novel's unique vision of a sexuality in control of its own representation.

Although critics have occasionally remarked on the presence of lesbianism in Proust's early works, none has as yet noted the evolution of his depiction of female homosexuality. Chapter 4, "The Evolution of Gomorrah," traces the changing depictions of lesbianism in Proust's writing from his earliest published works in the mid-1890s ("Avant la nuit," "Violante ou la mondanité") through *Jean Santeuil,* his fragmentary proto-novel, to the *Recherche.* What emerges is a clear pattern of gradual differentiation between initially similar male and female homosexualities. Although lesbianism does appear in the early period as an evident stand-in for male homosexuality (which is absent per se from these early pieces), it eventually comes to represent a specifically female unknowability. *Jean Santeuil,* Proust's unfinished first novel, contains the initial glimmerings of this paradigm, which in the *Recherche* becomes so all-encompassing as to infect Sodom itself (in the person of Morel, who, much to his male lover's chagrin, may himself somehow be a "lesbian").

The final chapter, "Mothers and Daughters: The Origins of Gomorrah," addresses the question of how lesbianism comes to play the role in the *Recherche* of an impossible fantasy of reciprocated desire. I conclude my reading of the place of lesbianism in Proust's work by identifying the origin of the "Gomorrah" paradigm of hermetic relations between women in the couple formed by the narrator's mother and grandmother. Proust has always been characterized as mother-haunted, and critics have universally assumed that the narrator's beloved grandmother in the *Recherche* is simply a transposition of the author's mother, with a few elements of his maternal grandmother added. One question that has seldom been addressed is why he felt the need to split the maternal figure in two. The bond between the grandmother and mother expresses its erotic potential through citations of Mme de Sévigné's passionate letters to her daughter. Their constant references to the seventeenth-century letter writer's life and writing establish a familial dynamic that anticipates Gomorrah, from which the narrator is excluded by virtue of his gender and implicitly relegated to the status of impotent onlooker à la Charles de Sévigné, the letter writer's hapless son. Here I use literary history, biography, and psychoanalytic theory to examine the role of the mother in the novel's account of female sexuality. I argue that the place of lesbianism in the *Recherche,* one of the least understood aspects of Proust's work, is best read in the context of what is perhaps the best-known facet of Proustian psychology: the importance of the mother.

This volume is meant as a contribution to queer theory and to literary historiography and also as a new reading of Proust's work in the light of his depiction of female homosexuality. In terms of epistemological focus, and indeed of sheer verbiage, Proust's preoccupation with Gomorrah in the *Recherche* dwarfs his much-discussed account of Sodom, and dwarfs too the meditations on time and memory for which the novel is most famous. Why, then, has this aspect of the work received so little critical attention? His representation of lesbianism has never entirely been given its due, either in traditional readings that dismiss it as part and parcel of the author's veiled portrayal of his own homosexuality, or in recent "queer-positive" re-readings, which, while focusing on a reevaluation of marginal categories, ironically tend to relegate Proust's treatment of female sexuality once again to the margins.[3] My aim is to answer this question and to redress the imbalance, revealing the centrality of lesbianism as sexual obsession and aesthetic model in *À la recherche du temps perdu,* and as epistemological blind spot both in the novel and in the history of its reception.

In the process, I have tried to provide a framework in which to reexamine the Pussy Galore scenario, centered on the figure of an eternally desirable, usually not quite attainable lesbian, of whom Albertine is one of the many avatars. The name Ian Fleming chose for his character—and which is left unglossed in both novel and film—goes, I believe, to the heart of the matter. The image of the lesbian represents, in *Goldfinger* and popular culture in general as well as in Proust's *Recherche,* a sort of femininity squared, a female sexuality so hyberbolic as to spill over into something else—a something that often gets construed, for want of a different category, as masculinity. The name Pussy Galore is successively understood as an interdiction, a challenge, and a gift withheld and then ultimately delivered. The lure of James Bond as a character is that he represents the impossibly phallic man who can win the impossible prize represented by Pussy Galore. One of the most remarkable, and underexplored, aspects of Proust's text is the way it examines this same myth of female impenetrability without resorting to a phallic solution.

3. There are, of course, exceptions, and I hope to make clear in the pages that follow my intellectual debt to those whose readings of the place of lesbianism in Proust's writing have made possible my own, in particular, Leo Bersani, Margaret Gray, Eve Kosofsky Sedgwick, and Kaja Silverman.

1

Sexual / Textual Inversion

Although the narrator of *À la recherche du temps perdu* engages in a great deal of speculation about various female characters' sexual preferences, remarkably little critical attention has been devoted to the question of Proust's representation of lesbianism. This neglect results, it would seem, from the fact that female sexuality in general has been taken as nonexistent in Proust's work: it has been read as male sexuality in disguise.

Or, rather, in several disguises. Proust's treatment of lesbianism, or Gomorrah, has been viewed chiefly through the lenses of two complementary truisms. The first is internal to the work, and it involves the idea that male and female homosexuality, Sodom and Gomorrah, are, as the title of the volume that bears their names suggests, parallel phenomena. To explain Sodom, therefore, as Proust's narrator does at the beginning of that volume, is necessarily to explain Gomorrah as well.

The second critical truism about Gomorrah is external to the work, although it takes its cue from Proust, and it has informed Proust criticism since the publication of the first part of *Sodome et Gomorrhe* in 1921. This idea may be termed the transposition theory, after Justin O'Brien's influential 1949 essay "Albertine the Ambiguous: Notes on Proust's Transposition of the Sexes."[1]

1. Justin O'Brien, "Albertine the Ambiguous: Notes on Proust's Transposition of Sexes," *PMLA* 64 (December 1949), 933–52; subsequently cited in the text.

It holds that the female characters in the *Recherche* whose sexuality is in question, notably the "jeunes filles en fleurs" who lend their epithet to the title of the second volume, are in reality young men; that is, these characters are based on male, not female, acquaintances of the author. Thus Proust, himself a homosexual, got around the problem of writing a semi-autobiographical novel featuring a purportedly heterosexual narrator by dressing up his own male objects of love and desire as female characters. Thus, according to the transposition theory, the reader must realize that many of the novel's female characters are actually male characters in textual drag, and therefore retranslate back into male, homosexual terms the elements that O'Brien and others, including André Gide and Jean Cocteau, have deemed discordant as presented in the book in female, heterosexual terms.[2] It is as though Proust were parading before the bemused reader a series of hairy thugs in sundresses.

Although both these readings, the symmetry model and the transposition model, are misreadings, they have textual as well as extratextual support. The idea of Gomorrah as parallel to Sodom is both suggested and tacitly disproved within the text. The reason for this apparent contradiction lies in the idiosyncratic nature of Proust's novel, which constantly juxtaposes diegetic material (narration and description) with expository passages, ranging from the aphoristic to the prolix, which implicitly serve to explain the narrative from which they arise. This is nowhere more jarringly evident than in *Sodome et Gomorrhe,* which opens with a series of revelations concerning male homosexuality, followed by a lengthy disquisition on the subject. The hero observes two male characters' discovery of their complementary erotic tastes, which leads to his own sudden under-

2. In the *Journal,* especially in several entries for May 1921, Gide discusses Proust's transpositions, noting that Proust himself admitted to having placed " *'à l'ombre des jeunes filles'* all the attractive, affectionate, and charming elements contained in his homosexual recollections, so that for *Sodome* he is left nothing but the grotesque and the abject." *The Journals of André Gide,* trans. Justin O'Brien, 4 vols. (New York: Knopf, 1948), 2:267. O'Brien, it should be noted, knew Gide and was his biographer as well as his translator. See Justin O'Brien, *Portrait of André Gide* (New York: McGraw-Hill, 1964). For Cocteau's observations on Proust's gender transposition, see *Past Tense: The Cocteau Diaries,* trans. Richard Howard (New York: Harcourt Brace Jovanovich, 1987), esp. 220–29.

standing of their sexuality, occasioning in turn some thirty pages of theo-
rizing about what Proust terms "inversion." This expository section, which
purports to unveil general truths, deals only in the most tangential way
with women (citing, for instance, the case of male inverts who are attracted to masculine women). Lesbianism is never theorized in the novel as
male homosexuality is; the apparent parallelism between Sodom and Gomorrah does not go much farther than the title. The volume opens with
Sodom and concludes with Gomorrah, but there the symmetry ends.

Since Gomorrah is never accorded a separate theoretical treatment in
the novel, readers have not surprisingly assumed that the narrator's seemingly conclusive findings about Sodom may be applied with equal valid-
ity to its female counterpart. This is not, however, the case. As is to a much
lesser extent true of Sodom as well, a careful comparison between the
(implied) theory and (apparent) practice of Gomorrah in the novel yields
enormous discrepancies.

In a nutshell, the theory of "inversion" that Proust borrows from
nineteenth-century sexology, and that can be boiled down to the formula
"anima muliebris in corpore virili inclusa" (a woman's soul enclosed in the
body of a man) holds true (to the extent that it holds true at all) for men
only. Karl Heinrich Ulrichs, the nineteenth-century German sexologist, ju-
rist, and Latinist who coined the phrase in question, also posited its female
equivalent, "anima virilis in corpore muliebri inclusa," but this creature, the
female invert, is nowhere to be found in the *Recherche,* nor is the term (*invertie*) that would designate her. Proust's Gomorrheans differ from their
Sodomite cohorts in that, in contrast to the men whose desire for other
men stems from their inherent and essential femininity, the women are not
characterized by what has since been termed gender dysphoria; they are
never truly "masculine," and they desire their like rather than their opposite.

While the figure of the female invert, the "anima virilis in corpore
muliebri inclusa," is not in evidence in the pages of the *Recherche* itself, it
nonetheless occurs in connection with Proust's work, in the form of the
transposition of sexes theory. If we are to believe, along with Gide,
Cocteau, Justin O'Brien, and many other readers, that the "ambiguous"
girls of the *Recherche* owe their ambiguity not to their taste for other girls
but to their extratextual origins as boys, then Gomorrah can indeed be
seen as symmetrical to Sodom, but not its female equivalent so much as

a different version of the same: men's souls enclosed in the textual bodies of women. This form of "inversion" is a function of reader response, taking place not in the text itself but in its biographically determined reception.

The discrepancies between Sodom and Gomorrah within the novel will be the subject of the following chapters. Here I shall deal with the transposition model of reading the *Recherche,* examining the degrees to which this approach is at once implicitly sanctioned by Proust himself and yet fundamentally flawed as a way of explaining the representation of lesbianism in his work.

The Transposition Theory

The transposition theory actually comprises two discrete, though convergent, interpretations. One, put forth by O'Brien in his 1949 essay and subsequently repeated by various other critics, centers on the idea that the portrait of Albertine, the hero's chief love object, is based largely on Alfred Agostinelli, a young man who served as Proust's chauffeur and secretary. Agostinelli eventually left Paris and was killed in an airplane accident in the south of France, events clearly echoed in the departure and death of Albertine in the novel.

The other version of the transposition approach predates O'Brien's essay, first appearing during Proust's lifetime. This reading is much less precise, consisting of a general perception that something fishy is going on in the novel in terms of gender. As Jacques-Émile Blanche first put it in the preface to the second volume of his *Propos de peintre* in 1921, Proust's text reads as though "there were a partial substitution of 'gender,' so that one could say *he* instead of *she,* and change all the adjectives that describe a character, his stance and gestures, from masculine to feminine."[3]

---

3. Jacques-Émile Blanche, *Propos de peintre,* quoted in Antoine Compagnon, "Notice" to *Sodome et Gomorrhe,* 3:1255, n.4. Like other commentators, Blanche seems to suggest a transposition not only from male models to female characters but also vice versa; it is not clear exactly what he has in mind, unless this apparent symmetry is meant to attenuate the implication of Proust's homosexuality.

Blanche, a longtime friend of Proust and painter of a famous portrait of the author as a young man, considers this aspect of the work "an added subtlety," but the allegation was not always made in such a charitable spirit, nor was it taken kindly, even coming from Blanche.[4] Jean Schlumberger, for instance, wrote a favorable review of the second volume of *Sodome et Gomorrhe* in *Le Figaro* in 1922, comparing Proust to Balzac.[5] In the review he also notes a two-way gender transposition in the novel, "making of a boy a young lady or of a dowager an old man."[6] This statement greatly strained Schlumberger's relations with Proust, who replied with a polite but frosty letter conveying his disapproval of this approach: "Your sentence is perfectly logical and implies no ill will. But coming after so many absurd remarks on my young girls/men in disguise it seems to lend to a stupid hypothesis the consecration of your infallible wit and your great talent."[7]

Rumors had long been circulating about Proust's own sexuality, much to his displeasure, and the young female objects of the hero's desire in the *Recherche* were, presumably as a result of what was known or suspected of the author's own predilections, read by some as young men. While it seems plausible and even likely that the portrait of Albertine owes much to Proust's relations with Agostinelli, at the level of the text the transposition theory breaks down. It cannot account for Gomorrah, for if Albertine is "really" a man, what are we to make of her suspected lesbianism? Harry Levin, in his 1966 book on modernism, *The Gates of Horn,* begins to deal with this issue. Arguing against O'Brien's thesis, Levin suggests that once one begins to translate the female characters "back" into men, there can be no stopping,

---

4. See Eva Ahlstedt's extremely useful account of the early reception (1913–30) of Proust's novel in terms of its moral dimension, *La Pudeur en crise* (Paris: Jean Touzot, 1985), 91–92. Proust had exchanges similar to his conflict with Blanche with the critic Paul Souday; see Compagnon's "Notice," esp. 1254–55.

5. Schlumberger was a friend of Gide, to whom he probably owed his insights into Proust's sexuality, and co-founder of the *Nouvelle Revue française.*

6. ". . . faisant d'un adolescent une jeune fille ou d'une douairière un vieux monsieur." Quoted in Ahlstedt, *Pudeur en crise,* 91. As in the case of Blanche's comment, Schlumberger's second example is somewhat obscure, perhaps an allusion to Charlus's "feminine nature."

7. Quoted ibid., 92–93.

for "to argue that we should read Albert, for Albertine, raises more questions than it answers. It is tantamount to arguing that the most indubitable female in the novel should nonetheless be denominated François. If we transpose the sex of Albertine, should we not likewise assume that her most intimate friend, Andrée, was similarly a masculine André?"[8]

Although it is not clear why the Albertine-as-Albert formula should imply anything at all about the housekeeper Françoise (nor, for that matter, is it clear on what basis the latter earns the epithet "most indubitable female in the novel," unless it is because she cooks and cleans), Levin raises an important point when he invokes the problem of Andrée, who not only is Albertine's friend but acknowledges having been her lover as well. As he observes, if Andrée and Albertine are both to be read as men, "that would reduce the dilemma to a mere pederastic triangle without the taint of lesbian complications, and it would altogether eliminate the characteristically Proustian note of bisexual rivalry" (414). Levin points out that the theme of the male lover's jealousy of a female rival is already present in "Un Amour de Swann," and further that it is a theme long appreciated by Proust in Balzac and especially, as we shall see, in Baudelaire.

Eve Kosofsky Sedgwick, in her groundbreaking 1990 book *Epistemology of the Closet,* takes up where Levin leaves off in discussing the implications of the transposition approach:

> If Albertine and the narrator are of the same gender, should the supposed outside loves of Albertine, which the narrator obsessively imagines as imaginatively inaccessible to himself, then, maintaining the female *gender* of their love object, be transposed in *orientation* into heterosexual desires? Or, maintaining the transgressive same-sex *orientation,* would they have to change the *gender* of their love-object and be transposed

---

8. Harry Levin, *The Gates of Horn: A Study of Five French Realists* (New York: Oxford University Press, 1963), 414; subsequently cited in the text. Levin had already advanced many of the same arguments in a reply to O'Brien's piece, "Proust, Gide, and the Sexes," *PMLA* 65 (June 1950), 648–53.

into male homosexual desires? Or, in a homosexual framework, would the heterosexual orientation after all be the more transgressive?[9]

O'Brien's solution to this problem corresponds to Sedgwick's first hypothesis, insisting on Gomorrah as a mere by-product of the transposition of sexes: "If Albertine had been named Albert and Marcel had been homosexual, Marcel would have suffered intensely from Albert's relations with women. In order for the *travesti,* or transposition of sexes, to be consistent, Albertine *had* to be bisexual (945)." The clairvoyant certainty with which O'Brien offers this hypothesis is presumably based on the knowledge that Alfred Agostinelli had brought his common-law wife with him to live in Proust's apartment. In any case, O'Brien's suggestion unhesitatingly fails to take into account the troublesome specificity of Gomorrah in the novel. Whichever of Sedgwick's options one chooses, whole sections of the text cease to make sense, because the hero's jealousy of Albertine's supposed adventures with other women contains central elements that are not assimilable into any other gender configuration. O'Brien's reading can be sustained only if one ignores the many passages that insist on the inaccessible feminine sameness of Gomorrah. The hero feels excluded from—and by—Albertine's desires for other women because he cannot understand the nature of the pleasure they would take together, or even what they would do together. By the same token, he sees Gomorrah alternately as a foreign country to which he can never be issued a visa, and as a freemasonry with its own incomprehensible rules and indecipherable sign system.

Although the transposition theory as advanced by O'Brien and his followers may, in the age of queer theory, seem hoarily inadequate as a way to understand the *Recherche,* it nonetheless has staying power, persisting in contemporary criticism as well as informing popular accounts of gay literature. For instance, in her interesting and idiosyncratic 1994 book *Reading Proust: In Search of the Wolf-Fish,* Maria Paganini maintains that "the lesbian scenario itself" in the *Recherche* "functions as a

---

9. Eve Kosofsky Sedgwick, *Epistemology of the Closet* (Berkeley: University of California Press, 1990), 233; subsequently cited in the text.

transposition of relations between men."[10] Indeed, the idea that Albertine must be read as Albert (or, more biographically, Alfred) has become so ingrained in literary mythology that it provides the name for an entire strategy of textual closeting. In the section on Proust in a 1996 volume titled *The Gay 100: A Ranking of the Most Influential Gay Men and Lesbians, Past and Present,* the discussion of the *Recherche* centers on "what has become famous as 'the Albertine strategy,' whereby Proust's real-life lover Alfred becomes, in the novel, the female Albertine in order to disguise the narrator 'Marcel's' sexuality."[11] Similarly, the entry under "Censorship" in *The Gay and Lesbian Literary Heritage* notes that "the most famous sexual transposition in twentieth-century Western literature involves Albertine of Marcel Proust's *Remembrance of Things Past.*"[12]

This view may fit in with current trends toward "re-gaying" homosexual literature of the past, but it entirely skirts the specificity of Proust's text. Both homophobic and gay-positive attempts to read Proust's women as men paradoxically have in common the effect of reading out of the *Recherche* what is perhaps its queerest aspect: the narrator's preoccupation with lesbianism. Taking the novel's sexual politics as dominated by an "Albertine strategy"—that is, seeing Gomorrah simply as a transposition of relations between men—does not solve the enigma posed by Albertine herself: not the question of the "true nature" of her desires, the enigma explicitly set forth in the text, but the related problem of why this becomes the novel's central issue. Furthermore, whether or not Gomorrah represents some other version of Sodom, either within the text or by biographical projection, the ques-

10. Maria Paganini, *Reading Proust: In Search of the Wolf-Fish* (Minneapolis: University of Minnesota Press, 1994), 46.

11. Paul Russell, *The Gay 100: A Ranking of the Most Influential Gay Men and Lesbians, Past and Present* (Secaucus, N.J.: Citadel Press, 1996), 129. Russell parenthetically acknowledges that this straightforward transposition is complicated by Albertine's lesbianism, but leaves the matter at that.

12. The author of this entry does, however, go on to specify that "unlike in simple pronoun substitution, Albertine is not just a camouflaged male, nor should her relationship with the narrator be seen as a homosexual one in disguise." See Joseph Cady, "Censorship," in *The Gay and Lesbian Literary Heritage,* ed. Claude J. Summers (New York: Henry Holt, 1995), 153.

tion remains of the relation between the two cities of the plain, and the hero's investment in each.

Baudelaire and Vigny

Proust himself, in an essay on Baudelaire and in a discussion recorded in André Gide's *Journal* from the same period, seems to have provided something of an answer (or perhaps two answers) to the question why a male author would have returned obsessively to the subject of erotic relations between women.

In an article titled "À propos de Baudelaire" which first appeared in *La Nouvelle Revue française* in June 1921, Proust devotes special attention to the "Pièces condamnées." These six poems were removed from *les Fleurs du mal* at the time of Baudelaire's obscenity trial in 1857 and not restored to the volume until many years later (indeed, even now in most editions they are set apart from the rest of the poems). Proust argues for the centrality of these works to Baudelaire's oeuvre, citing in particular the two lesbian poems, "Lesbos" and "Femmes damnées" ("Delphine et Hippolyte"). "These poems," he observes, "were not there on the same basis as the others, but for Baudelaire they were so much the main items that he initially wanted to call the whole volume not *Les Fleurs du mal* but *Les Lesbiennes.*"[13]

Proust then turns to the problem of what lesbianism meant to Baudelaire, given its evident importance in his work: "Why was he so particularly interested in lesbians as to want to name his whole splendid work after them?" (632).[14] In order to answer this question, he contrasts Baudelaire's attitude with that of Alfred de Vigny, citing the line from the latter's

---

13. Marcel Proust, "À propos de Baudelaire," in *Contre Sainte-Beuve* (Paris: Gallimard, 1971), 632; subsequently cited in the text.

14. Proust has not been the only commentator to ask this question (although he is one of the few to find the answer limpidly evident). According to Martin Turnell in his 1954 book on the poet, for instance, "Baudelaire's interest in Lesbianism is something of a mystery and no one has yet accounted satisfactorily for the prominence given to it in his poetry." Martin Turnell, *Baudelaire: A Study of His Poetry* (New York: New Directions, 1972), 204–5.

"Colère de Samson" which figures as the epigraph to part one of *Sodome et Gomorrhe:* "La Femme aura Gomorrhe et l'Homme aura Sodome" (Woman will have Gomorrah and Man will have Sodom).[15] The first part of *Sodome et Gomorrhe I* had appeared in bookstores only a few months before this essay was published. Given the volume's title and its epigraph, Proust presumably anticipated that readers of his essay on Baudelaire would make the connection—especially given the attention he devotes to Baudelaire's own early choice of title—and assume that the author was implicitly placing his text on the side of Vigny in his contrastive comparison of Gomorrah (Vigny's account of female homoeroticism) with Lesbos (that of Baudelaire).

Despite the fact that Vigny's poem itself does not actually address homosexuality of any stripe—it is, rather, an indictment of female perfidy in the person of Delilah—Proust constructs an entire theory of Sodom and Gomorrah around the lines he excerpts. For Vigny, according to Proust, Sodom and Gomorrah are irreconcilable enemies, as is made clear by two other lines from "La Colère de Samson" which Proust quotes here as well as in the opening pages of the first section of *Sodome et Gomorrhe:* "Et se jetant de loin un regard irrité / Les deux sexes mourront chacun de son côté" (And glancing with irritation at each other from afar, / Both sexes will die, each on its own side).[16] Baudelaire's vision, Proust observes, is entirely different, as evidenced in the following lines which he quotes from "Lesbos":

Car Lesbos entre tous m'a choisi sur la terre
Pour chanter le secret de ses vierges en fleurs
Et je fus dès l'enfance admis au noir mystère. . . .

(As Lesbos among all men on earth has chosen me
To sing the secret of its flowering virgins
And I was admitted from childhood to its dark mystery. . . .)[17]

15. Alfred de Vigny, *Oeuvres complètes,* 2 vols. (Paris: Gallimard, 1986), 1:141.
16. Ibid. Only the second line is quoted in the novel.
17. Charles Baudelaire, *Oeuvres complètes,* 2 vols. (Paris: Gallimard, 1975), 1:151.

Proust concludes from these lines that Baudelaire has accorded himself a privileged role in relation to lesbianism, and he goes on to wonder exactly what that means: "How interesting it would have been to know why Baudelaire chose this role, how he fulfilled it" (633). This observation would have the flavor of the familiar heterosexual male fantasy scenario if the terms of this discussion did not seem to preclude just such a perspective. Proust specifies the role the poet has taken for himself as that of " 'liaison' between Sodom and Gomorrah." Heterosexuality does not figure in this scenario at all. Proust then notes that a similar function exists in the final volumes (as yet unpublished) of his own novel, in the character of Charles Morel, whom Proust terms "a brute," adding parenthetically, "in any case it's generally to brutes that this role is assigned" (633). Morel is indeed one of the most problematic figures in the *Recherche,* precisely because of his role as liaison between Sodom and Gomorrah. Proust disconcertingly concludes his discussion of Baudelaire's relation to Gomorrah/ Lesbos with the confident pronouncement, "What is comprehensible in Charles Morel remains deeply mysterious in the author of *Les Fleurs du mal*" (633).[18]

In a conversation recorded by Gide, Proust deals with the same subject and comes to much less perplexed, if no less perplexing, conclusions. Gide places the discussion on May 13, 1921, between the writing (in April) and the publication (in June) of "À propos de Baudelaire." This was also the period between the appearance of *Sodome et Gomorrhe I,* which because of its brevity and alluring promise of further shocks to come had been appended to *Le Côté de Guermantes II,* and that of *Sodome et Gomorrhe II,* of which Proust was still correcting the proofs. He had insisted that "À propos de Baudelaire" appear in *La Nouvelle Revue française* immediately following publication of the first section of *Sodome et Gomorrhe.*[19] Both the publication of the essay and the conversation with Gide thus occurred at a moment when the public had begun reacting to the revelation of homosexuality as a major theme in the later parts of the novel. Whereas Sodom had been introduced both as practice (Charlus's encounter with Jupien in the courtyard) and as the-

18. For a discussion of Morel's role in the novel, see Chapter 4.
19. See Compagnon, "Notice," 3:1255.

ory (the long meditation on inversion occasioned by that meeting), Gomorrah, however, had as yet made no substantial appearance, since the hero does not begin to suspect Albertine of lesbianism until well into the second section.

The discussion of Baudelaire's Lesbos thus occurs, as it were, between Sodom and Gomorrah, at a time when Proust was still working on the depiction of Gomorrah that dominates the last volumes. Because Baudelaire was such a central influence on Proust, in terms of his representation of relations between women no less than in the aesthetic realm, it is important to understand Proust's account of the poet's attitude toward lesbianism. In his discussion with Gide, Proust insists that Baudelaire must have been homosexual (the word used is "uraniste"),[20] citing as sufficient proof the same texts he quotes in his essay: "The way he speaks of Lesbos, and the mere need of speaking of it, would be enough to convince me."[21] What he publicly designates a mystery, therefore, is privately identified as quite clear.[22] Baudelaire takes on the role Proust assigns to Charles Morel because, like Morel, Baudelaire is a homosexual.[23] Proust sees a man's interest in sexual relations between women as the displaced expression of a sexual desire for men.

Or so it would seem. Numerous aspects of Proust's interpretation merit scrutiny. First and most obviously, let us remember that Baudelaire is generally assumed to have been impeccably heterosexual. His interest in female homosexuality, which must be read in the context of the lit-

20. The terms *uranisme, uraniste,* and its variant *uranien* were borrowed from Ulrichs (in German, *Uranismus* and *Urning*). For a discussion of Proust's preferred terminology, see Chapter 2.

21. *Journals of André Gide,* 2:265.

22. To the extent, that is, that any conversation with Gide could have been taken to be private. According to Henri Bonnet, Proust was unaware that Gide kept a journal destined for publication. See Henri Bonnet, *Les Amours et la sexualité de Marcel Proust* (Paris: Nizet, 1985), 31.

23. Morel's first name, one example from among a proliferation of characters in the *Recherche* who bear the name Charles or names close to it—Charles Morel, Charles Swann, Charlus, Charles de Montargis (an early name for Robert de Saint-Loup)—may be read as an homage to Baudelaire. With the exception of Swann, himself once the object of Charlus's desires, all these characters turn out to be homosexual.

erary tradition that includes his predecessors Balzac and Gautier (the dedicatee of *Les Fleurs du mal*), has also been ascribed to biographical reasons: like Proust's narrator, Baudelaire seems to have been drawn to women with a taste for other women. This predilection has generally not, however, been viewed as a manifestation of homosexuality in the case of Baudelaire, other than by Proust.[24] The latter seems for his own reasons to be subjecting Baudelaire to an extrapolation—from art to life—that is the inverse of the transposition approach to his own work. Many of Proust's critics had already begun to conclude that an interest in lesbianism on the part of a homosexual male author could only have been a displaced way of dealing with male homosexuality. In contrast, Proust decides that an interest in lesbianism on the part of an apparently heterosexual male author could only have been a displaced expression of his otherwise hidden homosexuality. In both Proust's reading of Baudelaire and the conventional reading of Proust, the literary representation of lesbianism is seen as designating something other than relations between women: it becomes a depiction of male homosexuality in disguise.

Proust does not offer further support for his theory about Baudelaire, nor does he seem to think that any is needed. (Gide, skeptical at first, eventually allows that Proust may have a point but leaves it at that.) Proust calls attention to the character of Morel in his own work presumably so as to avoid calling attention to its narrator-hero, and thus to preclude or deflect the same sort of leap of logic that he himself makes in his conversation with Gide about Baudelaire. Also, of course, in alluding in his essay to events in volumes that had yet to be published, he was whetting the reading public's appetite for further seamy revelations. In any case, even if we accept his leap of logic regarding Baudelaire, two things at least remain obscure. First, the parallel drawn between Morel and Baudelaire makes little sense, both because of the incoherence of an analogy between an author's putatively autobiographical poetic persona and a

---

24. Proust's interpretation has, however, produced at least one convert: in a discussion of Rimbaud in *The Mythology of Transgression: Homosexuality as Metaphor* (New York: Oxford University Press, 1997), Jamake Highwater asserts, "I don't think it is coincidental that Baudelaire was homosexual (at least Marcel Proust and André Gide said he was gay)" (153).

secondary character in a novel, and also because of the terms of the analogy itself.

Morel is a Sodomite who sleeps with Gomorrheans, which is why he can be designated a " 'liaison' between Sodom and Gomorrah." Baudelaire's poetic persona is never actually shown in sexual congress with the lesbians he describes, although something of that sort may conceivably be inferred from the lines cited by Proust in his essay:

Car Lesbos entre tous m'a choisi sur la terre
Pour chanter le secret de ses vierges en fleurs
Et je fus dès l'enfance admis au noir mystère. . . .

Even if we assume, however, that these lines suggest sexual participation in the lesbian mysteries rather than merely voyeuristic access, the analogy Proust posits still does not make sense. Sodom is missing: while Gomorrah requires its better-known counterpart, Lesbos stands alone. Whether or not we choose to accept Proust's view that Baudelaire's depiction of Lesbos signals the poet's own homosexuality, nothing of the sort is evident in the poems on which he bases his conclusions.

Second, if Proust was reluctant to advance his interpretation of Baudelaire's relation to Lesbos explicitly in his essay, why then did he choose to suggest it by comparing the poet to Morel in the role of Sodomite ambassador, or at least cultural attaché, to Gomorrah, a comparison that leaves his reading somewhat incoherent? For one thing, he seems to be implying that any interest in lesbianism on the part of a male author indicates homosexuality, which is certainly not the thesis he advances in the essay as a whole. In order to understand what is at stake in terms of lesbianism in "À propos de Baudelaire"—and therefore to begin to approach Proust's relation to his own forthcoming depiction of Gomorrah—it is necessary to take another look at the comparison between Baudelaire and Vigny that frames the essay.

Proust opens by saying that he considers Baudelaire "—with Alfred de Vigny—" the greatest poet of the nineteenth century (618). He thus sets the stage for his comparison of Baudelaire with Vigny, who are placed from the start in a relation of identity and rivalry. The lines from "La Colère de Samson" that form the epigraph to *Sodome et Gomorrhe* are quoted not once but twice, the second time in order to emphasize the contrast between Vigny's view of the combative relation between the sexes, especially the cities of the plain, versus Baudelaire's idyllic initiatory vision. When first citing the line, Proust specifies what he considers to be its unquestionable biographical origin: "It is because Madame Dorval's liking for certain women made him jealous that he wrote:'La femme aura Gomorrhe et l'homme aura Sodome.'"

Proust's delicate reference to "certain women" must be understood as alluding to the cross-dressing George Sand, whose intimate friendship with Marie Dorval apparently caused Vigny much chagrin. The implicit binary opposition between Vigny's and Baudelaire's depictions of lesbianism thus becomes clear: the first is grounded in heterosexual jealousy, the second in homosexual complicity. It is equally clear, because of Proust's quotation here of the line used as epigraph to the newly published volume of his novel and echoed in its title, that Proust considers—or at least wishes the public to consider—his own version as following the model of Vigny's heterosexual relation to Gomorrah and not Baudelaire's heterosexual link to Lesbos. In this sense "À propos de Baudelaire" can be read as a sort of *mode d'emploi* or reader's guide to the Gomorrah that was shortly to appear in *Sodome et Gomorrhe II* and subsequent volumes, in which Albertine's putative sapphic adventures become central.

Once again, though, the terms of Proust's implied contrastive comparison are problematic. While his explanation for Vigny's bitter depiction of Gomorrah may be perfectly sound—though, again, Vigny's poem does not actually deal with lesbianism—a similar biographically determined reading of Baudelaire's poems had long been advanced. "Lesbos" and "Delphine et Hippolyte," along with the obscure concluding tercet of "Sed non satiata," have often been interpreted with reference to Jeanne Duval, Baudelaire's reputedly bisexual lover.[25] As a result, the origin Proust posits for Vigny's depiction of lesbianism in heterosexual male jealousy could just as easily be cited (and indeed frequently has been cited) in the case of Baudelaire's lesbian poems, which are here read in terms of " 'liaison' between Sodom and Gomorrah."

25. This suggestion was initially made by Nadar. See Joanna Richardson, *Baudelaire* (New York: St. Martin's Press, 1994), 73–76.

Proust seems deliberately to have set up an opposition that he knows to be false. This becomes clearer still when we consider that he performs yet another misleadingly contrastive move in describing the role Baudelaire delegates to himself with respect to lesbianism. In order to set up his comparison between the poet and Morel, Proust quotes lines from "Lesbos" that display the poetic persona in a relation of initiatory complicity with the women he introduces. Although he cites Baudelaire's other "lesbian" poem, "Delphine et Hippolyte," elsewhere in the essay, Proust avoids mention of it here, for the very good reason that this poem belies his depiction of Baudelaire's stance in relation to lesbianism. The configuration he presents as though it were a definitive or immutable position on the part of the poet holds true for "Lesbos" but not for "Delphine et Hippolyte."

The events in the latter poem, as opposed to those in "Lesbos," are depicted from the point of view of a moralizing voyeur, the poetic voice whose commentary frames the scene. In this respect "Delphine et Hippolyte" subverts another of the essay's implicit oppositions between the visions of Vigny and Baudelaire. When Proust stresses the biblical framework of "La Colère de Samson," it is set in contrast to the pre-Christian context of Baudelaire's Lesbos. The same cannot be said, however, of "Delphine et Hippolyte," which, despite the Greek names of the two protagonists, is heavily imbued with a spirit of Christian moral condemnation. This can be seen throughout the poem, from its formal title, "Femmes damnées," to its concluding apostrophe: "Descendez, descendez, lamentables victimes, / Descendez le chemin de l'enfer éternel" (Descend, descend, pitiful victims / Descend the road toward eternal Hell).[26] We are far from the sunny inclusiveness of "Lesbos."[27] Between the poem's unambiguous title and its closing dismissal, of course, the reader encounters a voluptuous voyeuristic scene designed to titillate, served up

26. Baudelaire, *Oeuvres complètes,* 1:155.

27. In his book on Baudelaire, Walter Benjamin addresses "the antithetical orientation" of the two poems: "'Lesbos' is a hymn to lesbian love; 'Delphine et Hippolyte,' on the other hand, is a condemnation of this passion, whatever the nature of the compassion that animates it." Walter Benjamin, *Charles Baudelaire: A Lyric Poet in the Era of High Capitalism,* trans. Harry Zohn (London: Verso, 1983), 92.

alongside the self-flagellating regrets voiced by the young blonde victim of Delphine's predatory attentions.[28]

Taking both "Lesbos" and "Delphine et Hippolyte" into account, then, one can accept neither Proust's characterization of Baudelaire as emissary from Sodom nor his suggestion that, in contrast to Vigny, the author of *Les Fleurs du mal* necessarily or consistently saw himself in a complicitous relation to female homosexuality. The binary opposition Proust sets up in "À propos de Baudelaire" between, on the one hand, a relation to lesbianism determined exclusively by heterosexual male jealously, represented by Vigny, and, on the other, a Sodomite identification with it, represented by Baudelaire, collapses at every point.

Although the either/or reading of male approaches to lesbianism which Proust offers in "À propos de Baudelaire" does not quite make sense, it nonetheless anticipates the ways in which critics have tended to read Proust's own Gomorrah. The treatment of lesbianism in the *Recherche* has been seen either as a displaced expression of the author's homosexuality, just as Proust suggests (by implication in the essay, and explicitly in his remarks to Gide) Baudelaire's portrayal of Lesbos should be taken, or conversely as an expression of the hostile heterosexual incomprehension of a Vigny faced with his mistress's putative lesbianism or bisexuality.

The chief difference between most critical accounts of the role of lesbianism in the novel and Proust's interpretation of Baudelaire's Lesbos and Vigny's Gomorrah is that both the transposition and the symmetry approaches, as I have termed them, in the end assimilate Gomorrah into Sodom. This is also, certainly, true of O'Brien's dismissal of the importance of Gomorrah in the novel as a by-product of gender transposition, an explanation that manages to combine the Vigny and Baudelaire models while assuming a hostile homosexual incomprehension of heterosexuality on the part of the author.

If we assume, along with Gide, O'Brien, and company, that Proust's "jeunes filles en fleurs" are best understood as young men in the skimpiest of

28. It is interesting to note that "Delphine et Hippolyte" in fact resembles "La Colère de Samson" in a number of particulars, and therefore that a more fruitful comparison might have been made between these two poems.

fictional party dresses, then Gomorrah becomes nothing more than Sodom in drag. Likewise, if we fill in the gaps in the novel's elliptical depiction of Gomorrah by assuming a symmetry suggested by the title of the fifth volume, then once again we take Proust to have created Gomorrah on the model of Sodom. In the chapters that follow I will examine the extent to which this second reading of Gomorrah as parallel to Sodom is both implied in the book itself and at the same time impossible to sustain as a coherent interpretation of Gomorrah as it is actually laid out in *Sodome et Gomorrhe* and the *Recherche* as a whole.

2

Gomorrah and Sodom

In *The Pure and the Impure,* her 1932 examination of the varieties of sexual experience, Colette opens her chapter on male homosexuality with a nod to Proust. She celebrates his treatment of Sodom and deems it an impossible act to follow, before going on herself to devote some twenty-five pages to the subject. While discussing Proust's inimitable Sodom, though, Colette pauses to take issue with his Gomorrah:

> But—was he misled, was he ignorant?—when he assembles a Gomorrah of inscrutable and depraved young girls, when he denounces an entente, a collectivity, a frenzy of bad angels, we are only diverted, indulgent, and a little bored, having lost the support of the dazzling light of truth that guides us through Sodom. This is because, with all due deference to the imagination or the error of Marcel Proust, there is no such thing as Gomorrah.[1]

Proust's Gomorrah, insists Colette, is a product of his imagination. She seems to be suggesting that Proust has extrapolated what he does not know from what he does, fashioning Gomorrah from Sodom, lesbianism

---

1. Colette, *The Pure and the Impure,* trans. Herma Briffault (New York: Farrar, Straus & Giroux, 1966), 131; subsequently cited in the text. First published in book form in 1932 under the title *Ces plaisirs* . . . , the volume did not receive its definitive title, *Le Pur et l'impur,* until it was re-released in revised form in 1941.

from male homosexuality. The paragraph concludes, magisterially: "Intact, enormous, eternal, Sodom looks down from its heights upon its puny counterfeit" (132).[2]

Colette's expatriate American friend Natalie Clifford Barney was also unappreciative of Proust's lesbians. In a section on Proust in her eclectic memoir *Adventures of the Mind,* she writes: "After the first volume of *Sodome et Gomorrhe* had been published, I expressed to him my admiration of Gomorrah. He told me that in fact his Sodomites were horrible, but that his Gomorrhans [*sic*] would all be charming. I find them above all unrealistic! Not everyone who wishes to can penetrate the Eleusinian mysteries."[3] The basis of her disapproval then becomes clear. Whereas Colette feels that Proust has taken lesbianism too seriously, exaggerating isolated instances into a fictional collectivity on the model of Sodom, Barney taxes him with not taking it seriously enough, not recognizing its radical difference from male homosexuality: "Even comparing it to whatever he may know of 'the love that dare not speak its name,' Proust could not have had any contact with these mysteries. It is risky to substitute the one for the other: *the woman will have Gomorrah and the man will have Sodom.*"[4]

Both Colette and Barney see Proust's depiction of Gomorrah as inaccurate, and both conclude that its inaccuracy stems from its having been created out of whole cloth in Proust's imagination, based on an extrapolation from his experience of male homosexuality. Unlike Gide, Cocteau, and company, they do not see his Gomorrheans as men in disguise so much as chimerical creatures conjured up out of an imaginative leap that takes lesbianism as the female equivalent of male homosexuality. Unlike Colette, who, despite her same-sex adventures, distanced herself from such matters in her overtly autobiographical writings,[5] Barney does not

2. It is not surprising that Justin O'Brien quotes this passage approvingly and at length in "Albertine the Ambiguous," noting that "Colette, whose word bears weight, has clearly stated the case" (946).

3. Natalie Clifford Barney, *Adventures of the Mind,* trans. John Spalding Gatton (New York: New York University Press, 1992), 67.

4. Ibid., 67. I have altered the translation slightly for accuracy.

5. On Colette's slippery self-definition in this regard, as well as for a discussion of her reading of Proust's Gomorrah, see my "Colette for Export Only," *Yale French Studies* 90 (1996), 25–46.

deny that Gomorrah exists as a separate entity; after all, she herself reigned over the Parisian subculture known as Lesbos-sur-Seine. Instead, she warns that it is risky to assume a parallel structure between Sodom and Gomorrah.

Barney uses the line Proust quotes from Vigny's "Colère de Samson" ("La femme aura Gomorrhe et l'homme aura Sodome") against Proust, to stress the difference between female and male homosexuality which she feels is effaced in the *Recherche*. As we have seen, Proust cites the line twice in the essay "À propos de Baudelaire," and uses it as epigraph to *Sodome et Gomorrhe,* indicating that Gomorrah and Sodom are to be read in the *Recherche* as parallel phenomena. Both Barney and Colette criticize this implicit parallelism, but neither questions the degree to which it is actually played out in the novel. A closer look at *Sodome et Gomorrhe* and the later books of the *Recherche* suggests, however, that the parallel structure announced in the title of that volume and denounced by Colette and Barney is in fact not borne out in the novel: it is a symmetry in name only.[6]

My focus in this chapter is on the complicated relation between Proust's "cities of the plain." I argue that the terms in which Proust frames his depiction of male and female same-sex passion reveal that only in Gomorrah can we find a true "homosexuality"—that is, a sexuality based on an aesthetic of sameness—in the *Recherche*.

Sodom versus Gomorrah

In Proust's novel as in the Old Testament, Gomorrah figures as the unexplained counterpart of Sodom. The title of the fifth section of the

6. Many readers have continued to see symmetry between the two "cities of the plain" in Proust's novel even in the face of evidence to the contrary. Leo Bersani's treatment of Proust in *Homos* (1995) attests both to the powerful allure of such a reading and to its inadequacy: "I assume a symmetry between lesbianism and male homosexuality," writes Bersani in an endnote, "a symmetry that the text may seem logically to require but that in fact, as Eve Kosofsky Sedgwick points out, the narrator fails to establish." Leo Bersani, *Homos* (Cambridge: Harvard University Press, 1995), 197, n.7.

Recherche clearly refers to male and female homosexualities, and suggests that they are parallel and that the book will deal with them either together or in turn. The volume, as we saw in Chapter 1, was initially split into unequal parts and published separately, the very short opening section introducing Sodom appended to *Le Côté de Guermantes II* and the rest appearing almost a year later. This division might seem to imply that the second part of *Sodome et Gomorrhe* was meant to concentrate on Gomorrah as the first dealt exclusively with Sodom; such, however, is not the case.

Lesbianism comes into question repeatedly during the second part of the volume, as women of what the narrator likes to call *mauvais genre* (literally, "bad sort") suddenly proliferate in Balbec; indeed, during his second visit the Norman coast seems to have turned into something like a belle époque Provincetown. He becomes increasingly disturbed by the idea that Albertine, the woman he loves, might know such women, fall prey to their charms, or even already belong to their ranks. At the very end of *Sodome et Gomorrhe II,* these inchoate fears take on concrete form when he learns that Albertine has long been intimate with Mlle Vinteuil and her infamous nameless "friend." This discovery harks back to the Montjouvain scene in "Combray," in which the young hero watches through a window as Mlle Vinteuil and her friend perform idiosyncratic foreplay rituals, a scene that then comes back to haunt the text.[7] It is not until the end of *Sodome et Gomorrhe II* that "Gomorrah," a label never affixed to the Montjouvain scene, begins to be used to refer to relations between women.

The peculiar asymmetry between the treatments of Sodom and Gomorrah in the section that bears both their names can be explained in part by the fact that the two succeeding volumes, *La Prisonnière* and *La Fugitive,* were originally conceived as parts three and four of *Sodome et Gomorrhe,* but different titles were appended to avoid confusion. As a result, the volume now called *Sodome et Gomorrhe* seems to privilege Sodom at the expense of Gomorrah, whereas Proust's early vision of what was to be included under that title actually contained far more about lesbianism

7. I discuss the Montjouvain episode in greater detail in Chapter 3.

than about male homosexuality. The fact that what Proust intended to include under the rubric *Sodome et Gomorrhe* kept growing in scope, along with the role of Albertine, suggests both the capital importance of what the title designates and also the degree to which the double-barreled name was meant to correspond to a double-barreled inquiry: Sodom, represented chiefly in the form of Charlus's adventures, and Gomorrah, represented by Albertine and her cohorts.

A certain chiasmic relation is built in to the examinations of male and female homosexualities in the *Recherche* because of the narrator's very different relations to their central representatives. Albertine figures as the quintessential object of erotic desire, and the narrator's obsession with lesbianism, however wide-ranging—with the possible exception of the duchesse de Guermantes, all the female objects of desire fall under suspicion of having *mauvais genre*[8]—is always assimilated into his jealousy of Albertine. Sodom, by contrast, despite its central incarnation in Charlus, invariably appears as the focus of a sociological, taxonomic fascination, general in aim and scientific in nature.[9]

The *Recherche* is, of course, hardly unique in this regard. Gay men have long been subjected to "purely scientific" inquiry at the same time that lesbian images have occupied pride of place in more obviously pornographic investigations. In French literature, Balzac's master criminal Vautrin is essentially the sole antecedent to Charlus (as Charlus himself is keenly aware); Proust and Gide are invariably cited as the forefathers of gay male literature in France. As for Gomorrah, however, Proust at once inherits and helps to shape the tradition of representations of lesbianism in French literature, almost all—the prominent exception being Colette's *Claudine* series—written by men. From *Mademoiselle de Maupin* to *La Fille*

8. Even Mme de Guermantes is rumored in certain circles to have had "immoral relations" with the princesse de Parme (2:933; 3:295).

9. Eve Kosofsky Sedgwick deals with this distinction in the context of the categories of sexual act versus sexual identification rather than in terms of gender difference: "While the Charlus who loves men is typical of 'the invert' as a species, the Albertine who loves women seems scarcely to come under a particular taxonomic heading on that account; it is as if the two successive stages of homosexual definition, the premedicalization one of same-sex *acts* and the postmedicalization one of homosexual *types*, coexisted in Albertine and Charlus in an anachronistic mutual blindness" (*Epistemology of the Closet*, 232).

aux yeux d'or to *Les Fleurs du mal* to *Les Chansons de Bilitis* to the *Claudine* novels (and it is perhaps no coincidence that this series, Colette's only first-person explorations of lesbianism, was published under her husband's name), female characters who exhibit homoerotic tendencies invariably figure as objects of male desire. They are also depicted as responding, to varying degrees and with varying consequences, to that desire. This aspect of the tradition, so central to what I have called the Pussy Galore model, accords textual sanction to male heterosexual reader response: a man who is turned on by descriptions of female homoeroticism can always find himself in the text, for instance, in the idealized hyperphallic form of James Bond.[10]

Proust's portrayal of Albertine and company fits squarely into this tradition. At the same time, though, it also departs from the canon of lesbianism in French literature in ways that have much to do with the vocabulary of same-sex desire. What is in question is no longer Lesbos, the Hellenic girls' school with its occasional sanctioned (and presumably heterosexual) male voyeur-initiate, but Gomorrah, which can never be separated from its more famous male counterpart.

As we saw in the first chapter, Proust's version of lesbianism has always been read in the context of the author's sexuality, and in reading Baudelaire's Lesbos as indicating homosexuality on the poet's part, Proust was attempting to read his own peculiar variation on a theme back into the tradition from which he had borrowed it. The reference to Vigny that is meant to impose a heterosexual interpretation of the narrator's relation to Gomorrah paradoxically, because of the valence of the term itself, serves to emphasize its inextricable linkage to male homosexuality.

The use of the title *Sodome et Gomorrhe* to designate male and female homosexualities is itself problematic. Sodom and Gomorrah, as anyone in Judeo-Christian culture cannot fail to know, are the Old Testament "cities

---

10. In this the French literary tradition is entirely in accord with cinematic pornography as well as more mainstream popular representations. In hard-core pornography, for instance, a film billed as all-lesbian may both reveal and incorporate its target audience by means of a *mise-en-abyme* final frame in which the camera pulls back to show the otherwise entirely absent male viewer-participant in his living room watching the film on video.

of the plain" destroyed by God in a rain of fire and brimstone because they were the site of unspecified "very grievous" sin (Genesis 18–19). Genesis 19:24 tells us that both cities and all their inhabitants were the object of divine retribution, but the rest of the story as recounted in Genesis speaks of the first city only.

For centuries Sodom has lent its name to what the *Oxford English Dictionary* refers to as "an unnatural form of sexual intercourse, esp. that of one male with another"; the first example of this usage given by the *OED* dates from 1297. In France a law written around 1260 states that "he who is a proven Sodomite must lose his ballocks, and if he does it a second time, he must lose his member; and if he does it a third time, he must be burned." This law, which seems to refer to what we know as homosexual relations, goes on to mention women specifically under the same rubric of sodomy: "A woman who does it must each time lose a member, and the third time must be burned."[11] It is surely a testament to the intricacies of the subject that the law remains silent on a number of dicey questions: "A woman who does it" ("Femme qui le fait") suggests that the same activities are at issue (perhaps the reference is to anal sex in both cases?), while the very different meanings of the word "member" in the sex-specific penalties ("le membre" versus "un membre," the penis versus a limb) serve to emphasize sexual difference.

The category of "sodomy" has long done legal duty for both male and female same-sex relations, as indeed it still does in many parts of the United States today, although of course the penalties are generally less stiff for both sexes than in thirteenth-century France. Especially given this tradition, it is hardly surprising if readers have assumed that what is presented under the rubric "Sodom" in the *Recherche* also holds true for female homosexuality. Neither in English nor in French has Gomorrah given rise to a noun equivalent to "sodomy," certainly, and in English "Gomorrah" is not even associated with female homosexuality, except

---

11. "Celui qui est sodomite prouvé doit perdre les couilles, et s'il le fait une seconde fois, il doit perdre le membre; et s'il le fait une troisième fois, il doit être brûlé. Femme qui le fait doit à chaque fois perdre un membre, et la troisième fois doit être brûlée." Rapetti, ed., *Li Livres de jostice et de plet* (Paris: Firmin-Didot, 1850), 279–80; quoted in Claude Courouve, *Vocabulaire de l'homosexualité masculine* (Paris: Payot, 1985), 191–92.

perhaps among aficionados of French literature. (For proof that the term has not taken on the same meaning in this country that it has in France, one need look no further than the title of Robert Bork's 1996 book *Slouching towards Gomorrah: Modern Liberalism and American Decline.* The former Supreme Court nominee surely means to suggest by his title that the United States is going straight to hell, not Lesbos, in a handbasket.)[12] In fact, the tradition that links Gomorrah to lesbianism is a short one, largely a French phenomenon, and almost entirely due to Proust himself. It was Proust who put Gomorrah on the map, as it were, as something more specific than a shadowy sister city destroyed along with Sodom in Genesis: it was Proust who made Gomorrah a recognized euphemism for female homosexuality.

Vigny had, of course, already mapped out the territory in his "Colère de Samson," with the line made famous by Proust's quotation. As we saw in Chapter 1, though, Vigny's poem does not overtly (or even covertly, except for the implications of this single line) deal with homosexuality of any sort, and even if the line in question assigns Gomorrah to women, it does not carry the meaning within the poem that Proust lends it by repeatedly citing it in isolation. The term "Gomorrah," as Reginald McGinniss notes, began to appear in the context of lesbianism in France at the end of the nineteenth century, so that although it was not presented as entirely concomitant with female homosexuality until Proust, he did not invent the association so much as solidify it and make it a part of the vocabulary of same-sex desire in France.[13] In Marie-Jo Bonnet's 1995 study *Les Relations amoureuses entre les femmes,* for instance, this meaning appears as naturalized, and is even retroactively in-

---

12. Robert H. Bork, *Slouching towards Gomorrah: Modern Liberalism and American Decline* (New York: Regan Books, 1996). Bork's is, of course, only one in a growing series of titles playing on Yeats's famous phrase; predecessors include not only Joan Didion's *Slouching towards Bethlehem* (New York: Farrar, Straus & Giroux, 1968), but also Peter De Vries's *Slouching towards Kalamazoo* (Boston: Little, Brown, 1983), and Geoff Hattersley's *Slouching towards Rotherham* (Huddersfield, West Yorkshire: Wide Shirt Press, 1989).

13. See Reginald McGinniss's useful article "L'Inconnaissable Gomorrhe: à propos d'*Albertine disparue,*" *Romanic Review* 81, 1 (January 1990), 92–104. He cites, among other examples, Victor Joze's 1894 *Paris-Gomorrhe,* which contained a chapter on lesbianism but the title of which did not designate that vice in particular (92, n.2).

voked in the author's explanation of lesbian invisibility: "The fact is that for Christian culture the lesbian does not exist, since Gomorrah, associated with Sodom in the Bible, disappears completely from the horizon of the Middle Ages, unlike Sodom, which is recognized, identified, described, and attacked by the Church, which sees in it a 'sin or crime against nature.' "[14]

Although Bonnet's useful—and unique—study of lesbianism in French culture does its part to dispel the invisibility she describes, this passage begs the question of silence surrounding the biblical Gomorrah, which had never formally, or even informally, been associated with sexual relations between women before the late nineteenth century. That its place is now assured, in French at least, not just as a vague suburb of Sodom but as its female counterpart, is largely due to the influence of the *Recherche*.

Inversion and Homosexuality

The vocabulary problems of "Gomorrah" do not stop at the title of the fifth volume of the *Recherche*. Proust avoids the term *homosexualité* in the novel, although, as with *lesbienne,* he uses it in his letters and notebooks. In the *Recherche,* too, it appears from time to time, but generally not without various qualifications that call attention to its inadequacy as a signifier.[15] The narrator refers parenthetically at one point, for instance, to "what is sometimes, most ineptly, termed homosexuality" (2:629; 3:9), and the ger-

14. "Car le fait est là: pour la culture chrétienne, elle [la lesbienne] n'existe pas, puisque Gomorrhe, associée à Sodome dans la Bible, disparaît complètement de l'horizon du Moyen Age, à la différence de Sodome, qui est reconnu, identifié, décrit et combattu par l'Eglise, qui voit en lui un 'péché ou crime contre nature.' " Marie-Jo Bonnet, *Les Relations amoureuses entre les femmes* (Paris: Odile Jacob, 1995), 26. This book is a revised and expanded version of Bonnet's earlier work, *Un Choix sans équivoque* (Paris: Denoël, 1981).

15. *Homosexualité* and other terms that disappear from the *Recherche* (such as *Lesbos* and *lesbienne*) occur frequently in early versions of *Sodome et Gomorrhe,* with and without qualification; see especially the passage titled "La Race des Tantes" (Esquisse I, 3:919–33).

manophile Charlus less censoriously invokes "what the Germans call homosexuality" (3:309; 3:810). The use of these and other periphrastic expressions implies that the phenomenon in question cannot accurately or adequately be summed up in any acceptable existing word. The terminology of Sodom would seem to present almost as much difficulty as that of its female counterpart.

Not quite, though: the author does have a favored term, *inversion,* a word he uses to theorize, but not in connection with women. Proust felt reluctant to use in his novel the term he actually preferred, the Balzacian code word *tante* (roughly equivalent to "queen," although English slang also offers "auntie," which is the term Moncrieff and Kilmartin use to translate *tante*).[16] "Balzac, with an audacity I would love to be able to imitate, uses the only term that fits my needs," Proust wrote in his notes for the novel, adding, "*Les tantes!* one sees their solemnity and all their trappings in the skirt-wearing word itself."[17] Not being Balzac, and all too conscious that (as he puts it with some irony) "the French reader demands respect,"[18] Proust used the word, which Balzac had borrowed from underworld slang for his *Splendeurs et misères des courtisanes,* in his informal writings, but allowed it into the *Recherche* only in the sporadically vulgar mouth of Charlus himself.

Given the unavailability of *les tantes,* Proust makes do with *les invertis.* Despite its clinical overtones and thus presumably more inclusive possibilities, the category of *inversion* shares with that of *les tantes,* in Proust's characterization, the fact that neither has anything to do with actual women beyond the pastiche of femininity. The narrator generalizes about

16. Richard A. Spears's *Dictionary of Slang and Euphemism* (New York: New American Library, 1981) defines *auntie* as "an elderly homosexual male; also a homosexual male past his prime period of desirability [U.S. homosexual use, 1900s]" (13). *Tante* would seem to have a somewhat less age-specific connotation, although its derivation does suggest something of the sort. The Larousse *Dictionnaire du français argotique et populaire* (Paris: Larousse, 1977) glosses *tante* as simply meaning *homosexuel* (232).

17. "Balzac, avec une audace que je voudrais bien pouvoir imiter, emploie le seul terme qui me conviendrait. . . . Les tantes! on voit leur solennité et toute leur toilette rien que dans ce mot qui porte jupes" (Esquisse IV, 3:955).

18. "Le lecteur français veut être respecté." Ibid.

l'inverti, never *l'invertie;* no such creature seems to exist in the world of the *Recherche.* Nor does he ever offer the same sort of abstract pronouncements about lesbianism that he devotes to male homosexuality in *Sodome et Gomorrhe I* and elsewhere.

Proust's dislike of the word "homosexuality," a German import that had gained currency in France in 1907 as a result of the notorious Eulenbourg affair, stems not so much from its etymological impurity as a Greek-Latin hybrid as from what he perceives to be its inaccuracy.[19] An invert is not a man who desires his like in another man, as the prefix *homo-* suggests, but rather is one who, insofar as he is himself feminine, desires his opposite. Charlus approves of the Germanic term both because of his allegiance to things German and because the invert—and the baron is, at least in theory, the consummate invert—is mired not only in deviance but also in self-deception as to the nature of his deviance. As Proust observes in an early version of *Sodome et Gomorrhe I,* provisionally titled "La Race des Tantes," "He is obliged to live the same lie with himself that he lives with other people, since, being a woman, he is obliged to believe himself a man in order to please himself."[20] The true male "homosexual" cannot, and does not, exist: "A homosexual," writes Proust in his notes, "would be what an invert calls himself, what he sincerely believes himself to be." [21]

---

19. For a concise account of the Eulenbourg affair and its importance in the genesis of the *Recherche,* see Compagnon, "Notice," 3:1196–1202. For a fuller treatment, see J. E. Rivers, *Proust and the Art of Love* (New York: Columbia University Press, 1980), 118–52. Robert Vigneron was the first to explore the role of the Eulenbourg affair in the writing of the *Recherche,* in his 1937 essay "Génèse de *Swann,"* published in the *Revue d'histoire de la philosophie et d'histoire générale de la civilisation* (1937), 5:67–115.Vigneron argued that the Eulenbourg affair played a predominant role in the development of the novel, and it also helped inspire Justin O'Brien's later assertion that Albertine was based on Alfred Agostinelli.

20. "Le mensonge où il est obligé de vivre au milieu des autres, il vit avec lui en lui-même, puisque femme, il est obligé pour se plaire à soi-même de se croire homme" (Esquisse I, 3:927). Proust later suppressed the title "La Race des Tantes," but it has nonetheless proved so compelling that the passage in its extant form is still often referred to by it.

21. "Un homosexuel, ce serait ce que prétend être, ce que de bonne foi s'imagine être, un inverti" (Esquisse IV, 3:955). On the definition of the *inverti* and the term *tante,* see the early text "La Race des Tantes"; see also 3:1308.

Homosexuality, in this view, is nothing but a chimerical rationalization on the part of the invert, a self-invention designed to preserve the illusion of masculinity. As Antoine Compagnon puts it, Proust "conceives inversion not as inversion of the desired object but of the desiring subject."[22] Inverts, then (once again, always male), never desire their like; what characterizes them as inverts, what makes them desire men, is that they are "really" feminine. One of the hero's discoveries in the courtyard is the triumphant explanation for why he thought Charlus had earlier "looked like a woman: he was one!" (2:637; 3:16).

Proust inherited this view of homosexuality as inversion of the desiring subject from late nineteenth-century German sexology, especially the pioneering work of Karl Heinrich Ulrichs, who coined the subsequently oft-repeated phrase "anima muliebris in corpore virili inclusa" to describe what he called the *Urning,* after Aphrodite Ourania in Plato's *Symposium.* This term then achieved a certain currency in French as *uraniste* or *uranien.*[23] (*Uraniste* is the term used in Gide's report, discussed in Chapter 1, of his conversation with Proust about Baudelaire's sexuality; neither version of the word is ever used by Proust himself.)

While Proust had largely borrowed a popular conception of male homosexuality, along with its vocabulary, from theories recently propounded by sexologists, his portrayal of Sodom in *Sodome et Gomorrhe I* displeased certain apologists for homosexuality, notably Gide, as well as some self-appointed guardians of public morals. The former felt that Charlus gave

22. "Proust conçoit en effet l'inversion non pas comme celle de l'objet désiré, mais comme celle du sujet désirant." Compagnon, "Notice," 3:1217.

23. The term *uranisme* and its variants became popularized in France following the publication in 1896 of Marc-André Raffalovich's *Uranisme et unisexualité.* While *uraniste* is the term preferred by Gide, *uranien* can also be found in the literature of the period. Courouve, in his *Vocabulaire de l'homosexualité masculine,* notes that *uranisme* and *lesbianisme* are used by some authors during this period to distinguish between male and female forms of *homosexualité,* whereas others specify *uranistes-hommes* and *uranistes-femmes* (225). *Uraniste* or *uranien* thus functions something like our term "gay," alternatively distinguishing male from female homosexuality ("gay and lesbian") and doing duty for both.

homosexuality a bad name, whereas the latter were outraged that Proust had named it at all; still others allowed that his depiction was sufficiently censorious so as not to glorify the subject.[24] Proust himself anticipated such responses, writing in a letter to Gide in June 1914: "The enemies of homosexuality will be revolted by the scenes I plan to depict. And the others will not be happy either to see their virile ideal presented as the product of a feminine temperament."[25]

Gide was indeed one of the harshest critics of Proust's depiction of Sodom. In his notes for *Corydon*, a work on homosexuality that saw general publication shortly after the appearance of *Sodome et Gomorrhe I*, and in which he criticizes Proust's approach, he distinguishes three separate types under the general rubric *homosexuel* (at issue, once again, are men only): "I call a *pederast* someone who, as the word indicates, falls in love with young boys. I call a *sodomite* . . . the man whose desire is addressed to mature men." The third category is that of the invert, "the man who, in the comedy of love, assumes the role of a woman and desires to be possessed." He reserves his criticism for this last variety of homosexual, adding, "It has always seemed to me that they alone deserved the reproach of moral or intellectual deformation and were subject to some of the certain accusations that are commonly addressed to all homosexuals."[26]

It is clear where the controversy lies: Proust's model of the invert is the very type of homosexual Gide singles out as attracting bad press for homosexuality in general (whereas, it should be noted, contemporary American societal norms focus opprobrium somewhat less on the figure of the

24. Ahlstedt's study *La Pudeur en crise* provides an invaluable overview of responses to Proust's work in this regard.

25. "Les ennemis de l'homosexualité seront révoltés des scènes que je peindrai. Et les autres ne seront pas contents non plus que leur idéal viril soit présenté comme une conséquence d'un tempérament féminin." Marcel Proust and André Gide, *Autour de "La Recherche": Lettres* (Paris: Editions Complexe, 1988), 40.

26. *Journals of André Gide*, 2: 246–47. Gide goes on to identify, with evident contempt, a category of passive heterosexual men who "play the role of true inverts" with women and thus merit the epithet "male Lesbians" (247).

passive homosexual than on that of the pederast, a category for which Gide reserves special honors and in which he explicitly places himself.)[27] In the letter to Gide cited earlier, Proust defends his interest in inversion on the grounds of authenticity and originality: "I tried to depict the homosexual smitten with virility because, without knowing it, he is a Woman. I do not in the least maintain that this is the only homosexual. But it is a very interesting one and one that has not, I think, ever been depicted."[28]

In the *Recherche,* this type of male homosexual does indeed figure as the basic specimen, and is consistently referred to as the *inverti* (and sometimes simply as the generic *Charlus*). Proust's refusal of the term "homosexuality" in the novel seems to be founded on the view that what we know by that name, notwithstanding his protests to Gide, is essentially heterosexual. It is a meaning predicated on gender difference, per Ulrichs's formula, even while characterized by sexual sameness.[29] In *Memnon,* Ulrichs posits a female counterpart to his *Urning,* providing the appropriate Latin phrase to account for her, "anima virilis in corpore muliebri inclusa." The term *invertie* was also standard currency in French sexological literature of the time, representing what would now be called a butch lesbian. In the *Recherche,* however, no creature of this sort seems to exist. No "Race des Oncles," even if there existed such a

---

27. Cf., e.g., *Journals of André Gide,* 2:247.

28. "J'essayai de peindre l'homosexuel épris de virilité parce que, sans le savoir, il est une Femme. Je ne prétends nullement que ce soit le seul homosexuel. Mais c'en est un qui est très intéressant et qui, je crois, n'a jamais été décrit." Proust and Gide, *Autour de "La Recherche,"* 39.

29. Eve Kosofsky Sedgwick demonstrates that Proust's characterization of "la Race maudite" is full of internal contradictions and thus presents a much more nuanced portrayal of male homosexuality than is readily apparent, including numerous subversions, within *Sodome et Gomorrhe I* itself, of the inversion model which that section of the novel delineates; see her chapter on Proust in *Epistemology of the Closet,* esp. 217–20. Because the central focus of the present study is Gomorrah and not Sodom, I have chosen not to deal with the internal contradictions within Proust's portrayal of male homosexuality—thus, it must be said, committing a willful oversight similar to the one I have pointed out in Bersani's *Homos,* also in a note and also with regard to Sedgwick (see note 6 in this chapter).

term, is ever theorized in complementarity to the *tantes* (indeed, nearly all the many uncles we encounter turn out to be *tantes*).[30] The novel contains only one allusion to the mythic figure of the "mannish lesbian" who was shortly to be canonized in English literature with the scandalous *Well of Loneliness* in 1928. Halfway through *Sodome et Gomorrhe,* responding to the narrator's anxious interrogations about her relations with other women, Albertine declares: "If it had been true, I would have told you. But Andrée and I both loathe that sort of thing. We haven't reached our age without seeing women with cropped hair who behave like men and do the things you mean, and nothing revolts us more" (2:862; 3:227).

Although the novel features a number of exclusively lesbian women (Mlle Vinteuil and her "friend," the actress Léa, and Bloch's sister and cousin, to say nothing of Albertine and Andrée themselves, whose proclivities never become entirely clear), none of them corresponds to this description offered by Albertine as proof of her lack of interest in such women. Albertine's remark can thus be read only as a sort of red herring designed to throw the naive narrator off her track. Such women, she insists, repel rather than attract her; but then Gomorrah does not turn out to be peopled by such women. The figure of the *invertie* is a myth whose existence the rest of the novel sets out either to ignore or to disprove.

In this respect Proust's depiction of lesbianism, unlike his version of male homosexuality, is strikingly modern, avoiding the sort of butch-femme paradigm to which Colette, for instance, succumbs in *The Pure and the Impure.* Proust's Gomorrheans tend to correspond more to the type that is now referred to as lipstick lesbians (that is to say, to women whose style is more or less feminine, and who do not conform to a butch-femme scenario) than to the figure of the prototypical butch dyke to which Albertine's remark refers. The single allusion to this sort of woman in her disavowal demonstrates that Proust was quite aware of the mannish lesbian type but chose not to include examples in his work. It seems unlikely, given his descriptions of the "Race des Tantes"

30. See Richard Goodkin's remarkable chapter on "avuncularity," sexuality, and narrative in *Around Proust* (Princeton: Princeton University Press, 1991), 17–37.

in *Sodome et Gomorrhe I,* that this choice can be attributed to an aversion to sexual cliché. Instead, we must conclude that Gomorrah was deliberately framed as representing something entirely different from Sodom.

Boyish Girls and Mannish Women

As opposed to the systematic revelation of feminine traits beneath the apparent virility of characters such as Charlus and Saint-Loup, the women in the novel who are known or suspected to indulge in sapphic practices are generally described as being at most "a bit boyish,"—*un peu garçonnes.* The narrator's other favorite locutions, *mauvaise réputation* and *mauvais genre,* represent the degree to which lesbianism becomes naturalized as the novel's one true form of female perversion, since in any other context and in the absence of further explanation, these expressions would indicate not homosexuality on the part of a woman but rather heterosexual promiscuity. The narrator himself plays with this semantic problem in *La Prisonnière:* when Aimé says that Albertine exhibits *mauvais genre*—the untranslatable phrase is rendered as "bad behavior"—what does he mean? *Genre vulgaire* would be the standard meaning, the narrator concedes, but *genre gomorrhéen* immediately becomes the reviled and desired alternative possibility on which he fixates (3:79; 3:592).

In the previous chapter I suggested that the presence of female inverts makes itself felt, through reader response, in the form of the transposition theory which sees Proust's Gomorrheans as young men in disguise. In the novel itself there exists a type of woman who conforms to the "man's soul enclosed in the body of a woman" model, but it is a peculiar testimony to the degree to which inversion is an exclusively male phenomenon in the *Recherche* that despite their apparent masculinity, these women do not belong to Gomorrah. In *La Prisonnière* Charlus has an extended periphrastic discussion with the Sorbonne pedant Brichot about "what the Germans call homosexuality." Here as elsewhere, the baron uses the seventeenth century as a point of reference for his discussion of homosexuality, noting the proclivities of various figures at the court of Louis

XIV. His disquisition leads him to the Princess Palatine, wife of the king's notoriously homosexual brother, the duc d'Orléans (known as Monsieur). Using her as an example, Charlus subjects this type of woman to the sort of taxonomic generalization that the narrator usually reserves for male inversion: " 'Such an interesting character, Madame,' said M. de Charlus. 'One might take her as model for the definitive portrait, the lyrical synthesis of the "Wife of an Auntie." First of all, the masculine type [*hommasse*]; generally the wife of an Auntie is a man' " (3:308; 3:808). He then adds, "that's what makes it so easy for him to give her children [c'est ce qui lui rend si facile de lui faire des enfants]."

The meaning of this paradoxical and grammatically confusing last clause, with its repeated use of the equivocal pronoun *lui,* could just as easily be construed to mean the opposite of what the translators take it to signify: that it is easy for a woman of this sort to bear the children of a man of that sort because of the complementarity between the two. In any case, the confusion—inversion, in fact—of sex and gender roles here, mimicked by the syntax of Charlus's last clause, presents among other things an example of men who are better at being women than are women themselves. This idea becomes a leitmotif in the novel: earlier, Charlus had proven himself to have a keener feminine sensibility than his aunt Mme de Villeparisis, as evidenced by his appreciation of Mme de Sévigné's letters; the "Tante" is thus shown to be more of a woman than his aunt.[31]

According to Charlus's model of the *Femme d'une Tante* type, a woman who is inverted with respect to the desiring subject—that is, a woman who is "really" a man—desires not women but feminine men. The novel contains a specimen of this type: the duly *hommasse* Mme de Vaugoubert, whose first appearance in the novel has already occasioned the narrator's observation "Mme de Vaugoubert really was a man" (2:669; 3:46). Her "masculine air" has nothing to do with a taste for women; she exists in perfect complementarity to her husband. The narrator goes so far as to remark that this type has "borrowed from her

---

31. I will return to the importance of Mme de Sévigné for understanding Proust's depiction of female sexuality in Chapter 5.

husband more than his virility, embracing the defects of the men who do not care for women" (2:670; 3:47). At issue, clearly, is not Gomorrah but rather a peculiar subcategory or annex of Sodom. Mme de Vaugoubert is the closest the *Recherche* comes to depicting an actual *invertie*; she exemplifies the gender dysphoria component of inversion but does not exhibit a corresponding desire for others of her biological sex. Instead of a mannish lesbian, Proust presents us with a mannish *materfamilias*.

At the heart of the ostensible symmetry between Sodomites and Gomorrheans is a logical impasse. Extrapolating from the theory of inversion set forth in the opening pages of *Sodome et Gomorrhe*, we are led to infer that a woman who desires women must herself be essentially masculine, and yet such a model appears nowhere in the novel other than in Albertine's disingenuous protestation of innocence. The reason for this strange gap must have to do with the fact that Gomorrah represents impenetrability only to those who wish to penetrate, that is, to men who desire such women. "We imagine that we know exactly what things are and what people think," the narrator tells us elsewhere, ruminating on the impenetrability of Albertine, "for the simple reason that we do not care about them. But as soon as we have a desire to know, as the jealous man has, then it becomes a dizzy kaleidoscope in which we can no longer distinguish anything" (3:529; 4:100). The mystery must lie in male desire, the vertiginous kaleidoscope through which, only imperfectly perceived, Gomorrah becomes a tantalizing enigma bearing little relation to the sordid predictability of Sodom.

As objects of male desire, women who desire other women cannot be "truly" masculine because then the men who desire them could only, like M. de Vaugoubert, be inverts themselves. Proust's theory of inversion, which, following the model of nineteenth-century sexology, is based on an essentially heterosexual (i.e., butch-femme) view of homosexuality, does not and indeed cannot apply to women in the *Recherche* because they are never only subjects but always, potentially at least, also objects of desire. The fact that Gomorrah, unlike Sodom, figures in the novel not for "sociological" reasons but for purely personal ones also means that the

Gomorrheans depicted will almost inevitably figure at once as both objects of male heterosexual desire and as subjects and objects of lesbian interest. Gomorrah is the sole context in the *Recherche* in which the otherwise unbridgeable chasm between subject and object closes, because the
laws of Proustian desire, according to which "love" is predicated on the
beloved's essential indifference, cannot apply among creatures who truly
desire their like.[32]

Logically, women cannot follow the book's rules of inversion because
they would not then present a mystery, this too being a necessary component of Proustian love, of which jealousy is both precondition and en-
tailment. Nor could an *invertie* provide an acceptable (that is, feminine)
object of masculine desire. Mme de Vaugoubert, because she is "heavily
mannish," is interesting only taxonomically, in that she represents a spe-
cialized offshoot of Sodom. Her desires are not really at issue; such
women exist purely as a form of Darwinian adaptation to the needs of
their inverted husbands. In a continuation of the botanical metaphor
earlier applied to Charlus and Jupien, the narrator hypothesizes that nature provided the future Mme de Vaugoubert with masculine attributes
in much the same way that certain flowers imitate the insects they must
attract in order to reproduce.

32. Sedgwick posits the relationship between Charlus and Jupien as "the single exception
to every Proustian law of desire, jealousy, triangulation, and radical epistemological instabil-
ity; without any comment or rationalization, Jupien's love of Charlus is shown to be stead-
fast over decades and grounded in a completely secure knowledge of a fellow-creature who
is neither his opposite nor his simulacrum" (*Epistemology of the Closet*, 220). I would take issue with both the initial statement and its justification: although Jupien does indeed come to
an encyclopedic knowledge of Charlus over the decades, their relations are hardly a model
of reciprocal love or durable desire. Rather, Jupien's love for Charlus comes to represent the
indulgence of a geriatric nurse for an errant senile charge; he is last seen in *Le Temps retrouvé*
dragging the blind and paralytic baron away from a very young boy whom Charlus has attempted to seduce (3:896; 4:442–43). In the final chapter of this book I shall argue that Gomorrah is able to fulfill the function Sedgwick assigns to the relation between Charlus and
Jupien—that of unacknowledged exception to the laws of Proustian desire—because the
narrator construes erotic love between women on the model of the grandmother-mother
dyad. Not coincidentally, Jupien's love for Charlus enacts in the end a sort of parody of maternal solicitude.

Various other female characters, it is true, display a somewhat boyish ambiguity that seems to appeal to heterosexual men in the *Recherche,* thus providing fodder for the theory that such girls are girls in name only.[33] Albertine and her friends in the *petite bande* are described as *garçonnes,* and Elstir's portrait of Odette de Crécy as "Miss Sacripant" deliberately plays on sexual ambiguity, undecidably depicting "a somewhat boyish girl" or "an effeminate, vicious and pensive youth" (1:908; 2:204-5). Between Odette as Miss Sacripant in drag and Mme de Vaugoubert's ponderous masculinity, however, there yawns approximately the same erotic abyss that separates Marlene Dietrich from Mrs. Doubtfire. Gomorrah leaves off at the point where the *garçonne* becomes *hommasse.*

The word *garçonne,* as both noun and adjective, carried great resonance during this period, especially, several months after the publication of *Sodome et Gomorrhe II,* with the appearance of Victor Margueritte's scandalous novel *La Garçonne.*[34] Nor, certainly, was the *garçonne* phenomenon confined to France. In America the boyish girl reigned in "Flapper" form, and Quentin Crisp describes this figure in England in the 1920s, noting that she had little to do with actual masculinity: "The word 'boyish' was used to describe the girls of that era. This epithet they accepted graciously. They knew that they looked nothing like boys. They also realized that it was meant to be a compliment."[35]

Boyishness in girls during this era may have represented a certain liberation from conventional gender restraints, but it is not to be confused with any "real" masculinity, nor does it necessarily have anything to do with sexual preference. In the *Recherche* the *garçonne*'s desires tend at least

33. And hardly even in name: as O'Brien points out, "The very given names of Gilberte, Albertine, Andrée" are "readily feminized forms of masculine names" ("Albertine the Ambiguous," 937). It is interesting in this regard to note that early versions of Albertine and Andrée bore quite impeccably feminine names, respectively, Maria and Claire.

34. This novel caused widespread outrage and protracted debate, and Margueritte was eventually stripped of his membership in the Légion d'Honneur. On the scandal of *La Garçonne* in its historical context, see Mary Louise Roberts, *Civilization without Sexes* (Chicago: University of Chicago Press, 1994), 46–62.

35. Quentin Crisp, *The Naked Civil Servant* (London: Penguin, 1997), 21; subsequently cited in the text.

to include a taste for other women, as is also true in Margueritte's novel, whose heroine counts lesbian escapades among her various transgressive adventures. For Proust a clearly demarcated border between "boyish" and "mannish" marks the limits of both Gomorrah and male desire. This becomes especially clear in the single instance in which Albertine is described by the latter adjective. In *Albertine disparue,* when the hero receives what he erroneously reads as a telegram announcing that Albertine is not in fact dead but is alive and hoping to marry him, he no longer desires her, and suddenly the image he sees of her is that of "a somewhat stout and mannish-looking [*hommasse*] girl" (3:658; 4:222). Elusive—or dead— she is *garçonne,* lesbian or bisexual, and ever alluring. Resuscitated, available, and talking marriage, she becomes at once repellently *hommasse.*

What makes women such as Albertine and Odette eternally inaccessible and thus eternally desirable is specifically their status as desiring subjects whose desire is always elsewhere. This is the very definition of the *être de fuite,* the paradigm of the Proustian object of desire.[36] It is also what lies behind the appeal of Marlene Dietrich in her tuxedo (as well, presumably, as the lesbian scenes in heterosexual pornography). Such women seem at least potentially to want both men and women—again, because they are never really "inverts" but always truly ambiguous, in both senses of the word (that is, "obscure" and "having double meaning")—but what makes them impenetrable, what the narrator of the *Recherche* fixes on, is their desire for women. As Eve Kosofsky Sedgwick observes in *Epistemology of the Closet:* "All that the two versions of homosexual desire seem to have in common may be said to be a sort of asymmetrical list toward the feminine: Charlus is feminized by his homosexual desire, but so, to the extent that gender is an active term in her sexuality at all, is Albertine most often feminized by hers" (234).

The analogy between Sodom and Gomorrah, between what is theorized and what remains mysteriously unexplained, breaks down precisely at the distinction (never made explicit in the novel itself) between "inver-

---

36. "Even when you hold them in your hands, such persons are fugitives. To understand the emotions which they arouse, and which others, even better-looking, do not, we must realize that they are not immobile but in motion, and add to their person a sign corresponding to that which in physics denotes speed" (3:87; 3:599).

sion" and "homosexuality." Like characters in Racine, the denizens of Sodom are doomed always to want the very people who by definition can never want them back—heterosexual men. Quentin Crisp pithily describes this dilemma: "The . . . problem that confronts homosexuals is that they set out to win the love of a 'real' man. If they succeed, they fail. A man who 'goes with' other men is not what they would call a real man. This conundrum is incapable of resolution, but that does not make homosexuals give it up" (56–57).[37]

No equivalent principle of displaced self-abnegation obtains among the women in the *Recherche* who desire other women.[38] Gomorrhean desire operates instead on a narcissistic principle of sameness, and represents for Proust, who depicted inversion as the essential form of male same-sex desire, a fantasy of true, reciprocal *homo*sexuality. It is thus in Gomorrah alone, in relations between women, rather than between Sodom and Gomorrah, that we find symmetry in Proust's novel.

The central problem in understanding Gomorrah in the *Recherche* is perhaps most concisely articulated in "Un Amour de Swann," when Swann receives an anonymous letter suggesting that Odette's past is checkered not merely with innumerable male lovers but with women as well: "He knew perfectly well as a general truth that human life is full of contrasts, but in the case of each individual human being he imagined all that part of his or her life with which he was not familiar as being identical with the part with which he was. He imagined what was kept secret from him in the light of what was revealed" (1:390; 1:353).

37. Edmund White also depicts a similar state of affairs among gay men in 1960s America: "It seemed a tragic situation, because whoever succumbed to homosexual desire became immediately undesirable." Edmund White, *The Beautiful Room Is Empty* (New York: Random House, 1988), 34–35. Elsewhere he locates the demise of this ethos in the wake of the Stonewall riots: "Today, fortified by gay liberation, homosexuals have become those very men they once envied and admired from afar." Idem, *The Burning Library* (New York: Random House, 1994), 78.

38. In lesbian culture in general, the butch-femme scenario tends to produce a slightly different anxiety of inauthenticity: that the "real" woman, the femme, will leave her butch partner for a "real man." In both cases what is perceived as difficult to obtain or achieve is genuine masculinity; but nothing of this sort is evident among women in the *Recherche,* in which Gomorrah seems to be an anxiety-free zone.

Swann soon discovers the error of his ways, as he begins to realize that there is an inherent qualitative difference between general truths and specific situations, and between "what is kept secret" and "what is revealed." It is in this early scene that the particular quality of the heterosexual male lover's jealousy of a female rival is established: as Swann puts it, "It's so calming to form a clear picture of things in one's mind. What is really terrible is what one can't imagine" (1:397; 1:359). For the male lover in Proust, lesbian sexuality is the epitome of "what one can't imagine," of what cannot be represented or visualized. The anxious vertigo that Swann experiences becomes a major theme in the second half of the book, infiltrating even Sodom as a result of Morel's "lesbian" affair with Lea (see Chapter 4). The central idea is that the pleasure women experience with other women is something inconceivably different from what men know, and from what women have with men. As the narrator puts it at the end of *Sodome et Gomorrhe:*

> That other kind of jealousy, provoked by Saint-Loup or by any other young man, was nothing. I should have had at most in that case to fear a rival over whom I should have tried to gain the upper hand. But here the rival was not of the same kind as myself, had different weapons; I could not compete on the same ground, give Albertine the same pleasures, nor indeed conceive what those pleasures might be. (2:1157–8; 3:504–5)

This inaccessible obscurity of relations between women is enacted on a global textual level as well. Whereas Sodom is both shown and told, the object of an extensive expository essay embedded in the novel, Gomorrah is only ever glimpsed, and the reader, like Swann and the narrator, must guess at what is withheld on the basis of what is displayed. Presumably this means that Gomorrah follows the model of Sodom, but that analogy, offered in principle, is never borne out in practice.

Proust, Freud, and Sexual Difference

Swann's and the narrator's vain struggles to imagine what remains obscure on the model of what is apparent, and the reader's challenge, if

she is to make sense of Proust's Gomorrah, both recall another, more famous attempt to come to grips with the female enigma. Freud's entire
project of psychoanalytic theory and practice is based on the assumption that "what is revealed" provides clues to "what is kept secret" without in any way being its equivalent counterpart. Neither Freud not
Proust is known as a believer in any limpid correlation between "appearance" and "reality," yet both seem to falter on this point when faced
with the problems posed by the existence of women. In the 1925 essay
"Some Psychical Consequences of the Anatomical Distinction between
the Sexes," his first text to grapple specifically with the implications of
gender difference per se, Freud addresses the issue of extrapolating the
unknown—female psychological development—from the known: "In
examining the earliest mental shapes assumed by the sexual life of children we have been in the habit of taking as the subject of our investiga-
tion the male child, the little boy. With little girls, so we had supposed,
things must be similar, though in some way or other they must nevertheless be different."[39]

Freud, like Swann, the hero and the reader of the *Recherche,* has assumed that "things must be similar" only to be confronted with mounting
evidence that "in some way or other they must nevertheless be different."
Here and in his subsequent essays "Female Sexuality" (1931) and "Femininity" (1933)—the titles grow simpler as matters complicate themselves—
Freud turns to this problem of sexual difference. The basic distinction he
finds is that girls, in contrast to boys, do not perform a neat affective split
between the feared and hated same-sex parent who is seen as a rival and
the adored different-sex parent who represents the once and future object
of desire. Female development is complicated by the preoedipal stage, in
which the girl's central object of desire, like the boy's, is the mother. Unlike the boy, however, the girl must then give up this object, entering the
oedipal phase of attachment to the father in order successfully to attain
femininity. Similarly, hidden behind Proust's global theory of inversion
lies a specifically and exclusively female "homosexuality." The locus of

39. Sigmund Freud, "Some Psychical Consequences of the Anatomical Distinction between the Sexes," in *Sexuality and the Psychology of Love,* ed. Philip Rieff (New York:
Macmillan, 1963), 184.

gender difference according to Freud is analogous to what we find in the *Recherche:* women, unlike men, desire their like.

Central to the girl's renunciation of her mother and subsequent turn to the father—that is, the move from preoedipal to oedipal stage in Freud's scenario—is the penis. The little girl, the story goes, has "a whole range of motives for turning away from the mother," the strongest of which are her discoveries of her own and her mother's common penislessness.[40] She blames her mother for bringing her into the world without a penis, and also for being similarly ill equipped. "Her love," says Freud, "was directed to her *phallic* mother; with the discovery that her mother is castrated it becomes possible to drop her as an object."[41] Henceforth, the story of female development according to Freud is one of coming to terms, for better or worse and in various ways, with penis envy.

The analogy I have established between Freud and Proust breaks down at this point. To Freud's notorious question of what "woman" wants, he himself repeatedly and emphatically provides an answer: she wants a penis (though certainly the mere fact of his posing the question, albeit in a letter, and moreover of its having gained as much fame as anything he wrote in his works intended for publication, suggests that this response does not carry quite the definitive authority he otherwise accords it). Women, according to this view, achieve a greater or lesser degree of psychic equilibrium depending largely on whether they continue to want a penis for themselves or are willing to settle for a substitute in the form of someone else's.[42] The question that reverberates through the *Recherche* is, in contrast, what do women want *from other women*? "What else can a woman represent to Albertine?" has become his central riddle, the narrator ob-

40. Sigmund Freud, "Female Sexuality," ibid., 203; subsequently cited in the text.

41. Sigmund Freud, "Femininity," in *New Introductory Lectures on Psychoanalysis* (New York: Norton, 1965), 112.

42. Freud also, however, stresses the greater manifestation of bisexuality in women because of their change of object and what he posits as a concomitant shift of genital zone from active, phallic clitoris to passive, feminine vagina. Some women, he remarks, vacillate between masculine and feminine stances, and he suggests that "some portion of what we men call 'the enigma of women' may perhaps be derived from this expression of bisexuality in women's lives" (ibid., 116). Here Freud seems to rejoin Proust's depiction.

serves in *La Prisonnière,* adding, "and there indeed lay the cause of my anguish" (3:311; 3:811). He never finds a satisfactory answer to this riddle, which becomes all the more disturbing as evidence accumulates that what women seem to want is not a penis, and apparently has nothing to do with that organ.

With the exception of Mme de Vaugoubert, women in the novel do not assume consistently or entirely masculine stances, and they seek out other women rather than men in order to satisfy desires that the male observer cannot imagine, in ways that remain equally obscure. He cannot imagine them because he knows that, to borrow Freud's words, "things must be similar, though in some way or other they must nevertheless be different." He can only try to imagine female desire and pleasure on the model of his own, and he perceives some fundamental asymmetry between the two. It is this necessary difference that becomes a key obsession in the book, the locus of female specificity and narratorial anxiety.

Where Freud sees lack, then, Proust's hero imagines plenitude. Women of Albertine's ilk satisfy one another in ways in which he cannot satisfy them, and indeed which he cannot even imagine. Their desire eludes and excludes him, and he both wishes to penetrate Gomorrah and figures it as self-sufficient and fundamentally impenetrable.

Freud's writings do, of course, suggest a figure that would seem to respond to this definition: the phallic mother, the chimerical psychoanalytic *être de fuite* that is the fantasy trace of a universal infantile misapprehension. Freud seems to vacillate when faced with the precise question to which Proust's Gomorrah offers an answer: the question of desire for sameness. The little girl in the preoedipal phase (elsewhere famously termed "a little man") desires her mother in an active, phallic manner. "As she changes in sex," Freud writes in "Female Sexuality," "so must the sex of her love-object change" (197). As in Proust's exposition of Sodom, Freud seems here to subscribe to the view of desire as being always necessarily heterosexual in nature, à la Ulrichs. And yet, since he stresses that the girl's phallic choice of her mother as love object is largely dependent on the belief that the latter also has a penis, the unexamined global heterosexualization of his theory becomes at a certain juncture incoherent.

In any case, Proust parts company with Freud on this central point: whereas both posit sexual difference as hinging on an originary desire for sameness on the part of women as opposed to men, Freud insists on phallic lack as the defining mark of femininity. Proust, in contrast, in a work in which sexual difference is centrally defined as the difference between Sodom and Gomorrah, situates true *homo*sexuality only in women. The depiction of Gomorrah in the *Recherche* offers the spectacle of a positively marked narcissistic desire circumventing the principle of Racinian self-loathing which defines Sodom.

Proust and Colette: A Tale of Two Cities of the Plain

To return to the responses to Gomorrah with which I began this chapter: when Natalie Clifford Barney rejects Proust's representation of lesbianism on the grounds that "not everyone who wishes to can penetrate the Eleusinian mysteries," her indignation is complicated by the fact that she is in effect echoing the narrator's own main point. Barney's criticism, however valid it may be in terms of the representation of a reality to which she had privileged access, nonetheless accuses the *Recherche* of inaccurately depicting something that it in fact announces its own inability to depict.

Colette's relation to Proust's Gomorrah, while based on a similar complaint, is more convoluted. Her statement that "with all due deference to the imagination or the error of Marcel Proust, there is no such thing as Gomorrah" bears further examination. As I have demonstrated, the assumption of symmetry on which she bases her denunciation of the novel's portrayal of lesbianism while lauding that of male homosexuality is false. At the same time, though, her point, like Barney's, is well taken in the sense that the Gomorrah of the *Recherche* certainly says much more about the author's fantasy of feminine sexuality than it does about actual women.

Ironically, *The Pure and the Impure,* the book in which Colette takes issue with Proust's depiction of lesbianism, itself contains a vision of self-sufficiency that closely resembles Proust's Gomorrah. It appears in her chapter on male homosexuality, the section of the book introduced by her remarks on the *Recherche*. For Colette, men together display precisely the sort of hermetic disregard of the other sex that characterizes Gomorrah: "They taught me not only that a man can be amorously satisfied with a man but that one sex can suppress, by forgetting it, the other sex. This I had not learned from the ladies in men's clothes, who were preoccupied with men, who were always, with suspect bitterness, finding fault with men" (139).

Both the heterosexuals she discusses and "the ladies in men's clothes" ("les dames en veston"), as she refers to the lesbians she has earlier described at length (always appearing in self-deceptive, doomed butch-femme couples, much like Proust's Sodomites), are found lacking in *Le Pur et l'impur*. Only among homosexual men does Colette see erotic equilibrium; their comparatively idyllic relations alone approximate the "purity" of her problematically binary title. Colette's depictions of female and male homosexuality form a chiasmic parallel to Proust's Sodom and Gomorrah.[43] Each author situates an exclusive psychological plenitude in sexual relations between members of the other sex, rather like the little boy and girl of Lacan's anecdote, each of whom is able to perceive only the door marked with the sign of the opposite gender.[44]

Both Proust and Colette play cagey games of self-revelation and concealment in their respective semiautobiographical works. And yet, here too, the symmetry does not quite hold. As opposed to Proust's Gomor-

---

43. Colette nonetheless clung consistently to the idea that her own view of male homosexuality closely resembled Proust's. In July 1921, shortly after the publication of *Sodome et Gomorrhe I* (and ten years before the first abortive appearance of what later became *The Pure and the Impure*), she wrote Proust a letter extolling his portrayal of the (male) invert and insisting that her praise was predicated on having wanted to write a similar portrait. See "Colette écrit à ses pairs," in *La Quinzaine littéraire*, March 1–15, 1973, 5.

44. "A train arrives at a station. A little boy and a little girl, brother and sister, are seated in a compartment face to face next to the window through which the buildings along the station platform can be seen passing as the train pulls to a stop. 'Look,' says the brother, 'we're at Ladies!'; 'Idiot!' replies his sister, 'Can't you see we're at Gentlemen'." Jacques Lacan, "The Agency of the Letter in the Unconscious or Reason since Freud," in *Écrits: A Selection*, trans. Alan Sheridan (New York: W. W. Norton, 1977), 152. See also Jane Gallop's commentary on this passage in *The Daughter's Seduction* (Ithaca: Cornell University Press, 1982), 10.

rheans, the male homosexuals Colette describes in *The Pure and the Impure* do not figure explicitly as objects of erotic desire. For this very reason, Colette's narrative persona (represented as a figure of the author herself, as in many of her other works) is able to depict herself as a privileged observer: "I was faithful to their concept of me as a nice piece of furniture," she says of her attitude toward her male subjects, adding that she felt herself to be "absent yet present, a translucent witness" (138–39). Her fly-on-the-wall position affords her the sort of ostensible disengagement that Proust's narrator elaborately displays in terms of Sodom but never Gomorrah. In this way the neat chiasmic mirroring between the two approaches does not quite work, since the disinterest that Proust's narrator affects goes one way only, whereas Colette assumes a generalized stance of transcendent objectivity, tempered in places by autobiographical "confessional" narrative that only reinforces her assumed omniscience.

She explains her ability to observe and depict male homosexuality as it is, untainted by her female, journalistic presence, by invoking her evident sexual detachment: "But, up to now, were they ever observed by any women for the length of time they have been observed by me? Ordinarily a woman—and let's say, an ordinary woman—tries to entice a homosexual. Naturally, she fails" (141). Colette exempts herself from the category of ordinary women, and maintains that she is able to see Sodom as it is, by virtue of her willingness to let homosexual men be, among themselves, without attempting otherwise than through her gaze to penetrate their hermetic world. Any other approach would in any case necessarily, according to her, remain futile.[45] Proust's narrator draws no such distinction between the desire to know and the desire to possess: this is why his curiosity about Sodom is always presented as idle and detached, never as

---

45. Throughout her writings Colette insists that men do not take sexual relations between women seriously, often even encouraging them as diversion or spectacle (see, for instance, *Claudine en ménage,* the plot of which hinges on this idea). In contrast, she stresses in *The Pure and the Impure* that a woman whose rival is another man knows in advance that all is lost (132). (The *Recherche,* too, offers the spectacle of a woman's unrequited love for a homosexual man, in the form of the princesse de Guermantes's longtime passion for Charlus.) In any case, Colette's repeated insistence on this point goes a long way toward explaining why she finds Proust's Gomorrah so lacking in verisimilitude.

true desire. For him, the gaze is the chief instrument of penetration, and the desire to see is inextricably bound up with sexuality.

Because the protagonist of the *Recherche,* unlike Colette's narrative persona in *The Pure and the Impure,* fully assumes a desiring stance in relation to homosexuality in the other sex, he effectively creates something like a heterosexual version of what I have termed the Racinian dilemma inherent in Proust's Sodom. In Quentin Crisp's terms, if he succeeds, he fails; or, rather, a certain will to failure seems written into his sexual preference. His desire for Albertine grows in direct proportion to his conviction that her sexuality excludes him by virtue of his gender. In the next chapter I examine how this conundrum plays itself out in the novel's scenes of voyeurism.

3

Reading between the Blinds

The attention the narrator devotes to the mystery of Albertine's desires takes up more textual space than any other concern in the *Recherche,* and Albertine's name occurs more often than that of any other character.[1] Why, then—once again—has this subject been so relatively neglected in the history of Proust criticism? Malcolm Bowie, in *Freud, Proust, and Lacan: Theory as Fiction,* notes a "thoroughly disturbing, amnesic tendency" on the part of critics to ignore the more messily obsessive sections of the novel in favor of the familiar framing volumes which offer a prospect of redemption in art. Bowie points out that the least examined part of the text comprises *Sodome et Gomorrhe, La Prisonnière,* and *Albertine disparue*—that is, the "roman d'Albertine"—a lapse that "allow[s] the profoundly unsettling view of human sexuality enshrined in these volumes to be held at a tranquillising distance."[2]

---

1. Her name appears 2,360 times (along with 3 occurrences in the plural), as opposed to 1,643 mentions of Swann by name and 1,294 of Charlus; furthermore, *maman* receives only 210 mentions, although the word *mère* occurs 1,404 times. This information can be found in volume 3 of Étienne Brunet, *Le Vocabulaire de Proust,* 3 vols. (Geneva: Slatkine-Champion, 1983).

2. Malcolm Bowie, *Freud, Proust, and Lacan: Theory as Fiction* (Cambridge: Cambridge University Press, 1987), 46.

Here again, as in the reading of lesbianism as male homosexuality in disguise, Proust has shown us the way. The novel's concluding passages seem to support a reading whereby much of what occurs between the madeleine scene and the narrator's epiphanic moments at the Guermantes *matinée* is prologue, subordinate to the discovery of his higher calling. This implicit invitation to discount the inner volumes has long been taken up with enthusiasm, as is dramatized, for instance, by the availability of an audiocassette version of *À la recherche du temps perdu,* read by Jean-Louis Trintignant and consisting, on two cassettes, of passages from "Combray" and the end of *Le Temps retrouvé.*[3] The beginning and end of the novel were written first, and in them Proust saw the shape of the *Recherche* as a whole, announcing in a letter to Mme Straus as early as 1909 that he had just both begun and finished a long book.[4] Albertine does not begin to figure in Proust's notes until 1913.

The author thus sanctions critical neglect of his depiction of female sexuality at least twice over. As we saw in Chapter 1, he implicitly suggests, even while overtly denying, that his portrayal of lesbianism must inevitably be read as another version of male homosexuality. Also, he both privileges the frame of his novel at the expense of its contents and structures it so that what the hero has learned by the end allows him, and the reader with him, retrospectively to discredit the sort of epistemological and emotional distraction incarnated in Albertine. Roger Shattuck, for instance, in his award-winning 1974 study of Proust, declares himself interested in the "deep universal element, an esthetic consciousness," in the *Recherche,* which is doubtless what leads him to note that the entirety of *Albertine disparue,* the volume centrally concerned with Albertine's sexuality, may safely be omitted by the time-pressed reader.[5]

---

3. This audiocassette is published by Éditions des femmes, and contains the word "extraits" in small letters on the back cover, whereas the front announces only *À la recherche du temps perdu.* To be fair, I should add that Éditions Thélème have produced audiocassette readings of the *Recherche* in its voluminous entirety.

4. See Marcel Proust, *Selected Letters,* vol. 2, *1904–9,* ed. Philip Kolb, trans. Terence Kilmartin (New York: Oxford University Press, 1989), 446.

5. Roger Shattuck, *Marcel Proust* (Princeton: Princeton University Press, 1974), 27–28.

Gomorrah is represented, by Proust's narrator no less than by Shattuck, as a textual red herring, a false trail on the road to enlightement, to what Shattuck calls "esthetic consciousness." In principle, this should be true for Sodom as well. It is not, however: the sociological importance with which the observation of Sodom is invested acts as its own justification.

The narrator's consuming obsession with Albertine's sexuality, though it forms his most urgent interest, is presented as an essentially unworthy pursuit, because Gomorrah never transcends the realm of the merely specific. For example, while engaging in protracted speculation about whether Albertine knows the actress Léa and her reputedly lesbian entourage, the narrator makes a telling aside in *La Prisonnière:* "At this moment, the thought that she must not meet the two girls again and the question whether or not she knew Léa were what was chiefly occupying my mind, in spite of the rule that one ought not to take an interest in particular facts except in relation to their general significance" (3:147; 3:657).

Proust's emphatic subordination of the particular to the general, writ large at the end of the novel, clearly dictates that Sodom be taken more seriously than Gomorrah, since the former is consistently portrayed as an object of general rather than particular interest. In the very first sentence of *Sodome et Gomorrhe I* the narrator frames the courtyard seduction scene between Charlus and Jupien as not merely related gossip but rather the revelation of an intrinsically important truth, "a discovery which concerned M. de Charlus in particular but was in itself so important that I have until now, until the moment when I could give it the prominence and treat it with the fullness that it demanded, postponed giving an account of it" (2:263; 3:3). This claim for the larger implications of what is after all a prurient scene of voyeurism is then backed up by the extended expository passage referred to as "La Race des Tantes." The first description of lesbian relations is presented very differently, circumscribed by a specificity that seems to preclude its incorporation into any general system of truth, even though its placement ensures its importance in the grand Proustian scheme of things.

The Montjouvain scene occurs in "Combray," the novel's best-known section—in fact the only one sanctified for the American undergraduate classroom, thanks to Germaine Brée's annotated edition—and a privileged locus of truth production. The only hint of Sodom in "Combray" is so exquisitely subtle as to render the proleptic irony with which it is imbued entirely imperceptible upon first reading. When Charlus first appears, the narrator notes that he "stared at me with eyes which seemed to be starting from his head" (1:154; 1:140) (retrospectively to be read as the sign of his uncontrollable interest in boys), and the narrator's grandfather takes Swann to be a dupe for allowing Odette to disport herself publicly with "her Charlus" (1: 1155; 1:140). Such details are evidently meant for the delectation of enlightened re-readers, while remaining opaque to the novice.[6]

In contrast, the Montjouvain scene calls attention to itself both in the dramatically perverse nature of what it contains and because of its apparent misplacedness. It seems almost to come from a different book than the rest of "Combray," and indeed, in a sense, it does: it belongs to the world of *Sodome et Gomorrhe.* Proust himself was forced to admit this when, on publication of *Du côté de chez Swann,* influential readers protested what they saw as the gratuitous lewdness of the Montjouvain scene; the Catholic author Francis Jammes, for one, "ardently begged" him to remove it from the book. Defending himself in a letter to Paul Souday, Proust wrote that the passage

> was, indeed, "useless" in the first volume. But its remembrance is the foundation of volumes IV and V (through the jealousy it inspires, etc.). In suppressing this scene, I would not have changed very much in the first volume; I would have, in return, because of the interdependence of the parts, caused two entire volumes, of which this scene is the cornerstone, to fall down around the reader's ears.[7]

The two volumes in question, *La Prisonnière* and *Albertine disparue,* are, of course, those most clearly marked for omission by readers such as Shattuck.

6. See my essay "Rereading Proust: Perversion and Prolepsis in *À la recherche du temps perdu,*" in *Second Thoughts: On Rereading,* ed. David Galef (Detroit: Wayne State University Press, 1998), 249–65. See also Proust's letter to Henri Ghéon on the subject of this first appearance of Charlus in Marcel Proust, *Correspondance,* ed. Philip Kolb, 21 vols. (Paris: Plon, 1970–93), 13:25–26; quoted 1:1166.

7. Quoted in Rivers, *Proust and the Art of Love,* 24.

The Montjouvain scene thus bridges the perceived structural binarism between the serious outer volumes addressing the nature of time and memory and the trivia-infused inner volumes that deal with deviant sexuality.
Among other things, the fact that it was already present in Proust's earliest
version of the novel means that even if Gomorrah's prominence in the
book grew disproportionately as Albertine's story took shape, it predates
her existence per se. The placement of Mlle Vinteuil and her friend in the
most prestigious neighborhood of the *Recherche, Du côté de chez Swann,*
contradicts *Le Temps retrouvé*'s implicit relegation of Gomorrah to the role
of perverse distraction.

At the same time that its prominent location accords the passage great
significance, that significance is left unexplained, to function as the first
volume's most evident and yet most mysterious foreshadowing of the rest
of the book. The Montjouvain scene is planted, like a billboard advertis-
ing a distant landmark, literally thousands of pages from any contextual-
ization of what we are told will be seen "in due course" and "for quite
other reasons" to have played an important role in the narrator's life
(1:173; 1:157). He gives us to understand that the most crucial distinction
between Sodom and Gomorrah is that the former is "important in itself,"
the latter merely "important in my life," but the Montjouvain scene suggests otherwise.

Voyeurism and Exhibitionism

A comparison of the various scenes of voyeurism in the novel reveals
manifold differences between the narrator's visual and epistemological relations to Sodom and to Gomorrah, not only in what he sees but in how,
and indeed whether, he sees it. As Eve Sedgwick points out in *Epistemology of the Closet,* Charlus's "open secret" offers what she calls "the spectacle
of the closet," whereas Albertine's sexuality resists visualization.[8] Charlus

---

8. In *Epistemology of the Closet,* Sedgwick reads the unknowability of Albertine's sexuality
as allowing the narrator a form of closetedness that plays off Charlus: "Seemingly, Charlus's
closet is specularized *so that* the erotics around Albertine (which is to say, around the narrator) may continue to resist visualization; it is from the inchoate space that will include

hides "a secret known by all," to borrow a formula from Baudelaire,[9] and his and his Sodomite cohorts' constant inadvertent self-disclosure presents a sharp contrast to the enduring opacity of Gomorrah. In the novel's various scenes of voyeurism, the narrator is consistently able to witness spectacles of male homosexual debauchery in all their depraved grandeur, while each of his efforts to see what women do together ends, as does the Montjouvain scene, with the blinds being drawn at the crucial moment.

In other words, the blindness that critics have consistently displayed to the specificity of Gomorrah in the *Recherche* echoes the narrator's own inability to see relations between women. If he cannot see Gomorrah, however, it is not for want of trying. Nor, strangely enough, is it for lack of being shown: one of the ways in which lesbian sexuality differs in the *Recherche* from male homosexuality is that, in contrast to their Sodomite counterparts, Gomorrheans display a marked tendency toward exhibitionism.

Charlus's "closet as spectacle"—in Sedgwick's terms, his "glass closet" (228)—is predicated on his insistence on hiding what everyone assumes to be his ultimate truth. Since the truth of his sexuality is intimately bound up with his ostrich-like concealment of it, "the spectacle of the closet," as Sedgwick puts it, must be read as "the truth of the homosexual" (231). The nature of Sodom is not just the content of its secret but the nature of its secretiveness.

Gomorrah functions very differently. This is clear in the Montjouvain scene itself, which indeed stages a spectacle, but what is "closeted" is the narrator's voyeurism more than the women's lesbianism. The stated lesson of this episode, moreover, concerns not homosexuality but "sadism." That the book's introduction of this particular vice should purportedly occur only at Montjouvain may seem odd, since by this point we have already learned about various sorts of cruelty: even aside from the father's insis-

---

Albertine, and to guarantee its privileged exemption from sight, that the narrator stages the presentation of Charlus" (231).

9. "Un secret de tous connu"; see Charles Baudelaire, "Semper eadem," in *Oeuvres complètes,* 1:41. Baudelaire uses the phrase to refer to both *taedium vitae* and female promiscuity, but it applies with great aptness to the dynamics of Charlus's sexuality.

tence that the boy do without his mother's good-night kiss, the narrator
has previously described the family ritual of tormenting the grandmother
(1:12–13; 1:11–12), as well as Françoise's nasty treatment of both the preg-
nant kitchen maid and a hapless chicken destined for the dinner table
(1:132–35; 1:119–22). The term "sadism" in this passage, though, has a
more nuanced connotation of cruelty toward an absent victim.[10] It specifically refers to parental profanation, a theme running through Proust's
writings, usually in the form of desecration of the mother, and whose
meaning seems inextricably bound up with homosexuality: Charlus, for
instance, is said to profane his mother's memory merely by resembling
her.

The commentary around the Montjouvain scene fixates not on the fact
that the two people whose foreplay ritual the hero witnesses are both
women (explicit notice of this aspect of the couple is for the moment
confined to ribald remarks made by local gossips) but rather on the use
Mlle Vinteuil makes in her erotic games with her nameless "friend" of a
photograph of her late father, who doted on her and whom she is said to
have killed by dint of her perversion.

The "sadism" component of this scene, as we shall see in the next
chapter, should be read as a holdover from Proust's writings of the 1890s,
in which lesbianism doubled for male homosexuality. (It is also echoed
several volumes later, in *Sodome et Gomorrhe II*, when Morel titillates
Charlus by describing his plans to seduce and abandon a virgin; see
2:1040–41; 3:396–97). What is peculiar to Gomorrah in this passage is that
the young hero is able to witness the ritual erotic play between the two
women only because the idea of being seen is an integral part of their
sexual game.

Exhibitionism is written into this episode on a number of levels. When
the hero falls asleep in the bushes outside Mlle Vinteuil's house at Montjouvain, he is repeating a previous moment in which his disavowed
voyeurism has already been matched by an equally disavowed exhibitionism, masquerading as modesty, on the part of Mlle Vinteuil's father. Some

10. On the question of cruelty in the *Recherche*, see the chapter titled "'Ce frémissement
d'un coeur à qui on fait mal,'" in Antoine Compagnon's *Proust entre deux siècles* (Paris: Seuil,
1989), 153–86.

fifty pages earlier, hidden in the bushes outside the house while his parents paid a visit to M.Vinteuil, he had watched as the latter carefully placed sheet music on the piano in preparation for the visit, then insisted, in the face of the hero's mother's entreaties to play the music: " 'I can't think who put that on the piano; it's not the proper place for it at all,' and [he] had turned the conversation aside to other topics, precisely because they were of less interest to himself" (1:122; 1:112). This scene is repeated practically verbatim in the subsequent passage, after M.Vinteuil's death, when his portrait is substituted for his music: "Oh!" cries Mlle Vinteuil after placing the photograph in a prominent position, "there's my father's picture looking at us; I can't think who can have put it there; I'm sure I've told them a dozen times that it isn't the proper place for it" (1:177; 1:160). M.Vinteuil's own artistic exhibitionism thus comes back to haunt him in sexualized form as his image haunts his daughter; he is made both to witness his own degradation—his portrait will be spat upon—and by the same token to serve as a prop in his daughter's debauchery.

The *mise-en-abyme* audience which M. Vinteuil's portrait becomes is only part of the intricate circle of voyeurism and exhibitionism at Montjouvain. The hero is able to witness the scene between Mlle Vinteuil and her friend by virtue of a voyeuristic design that is at least as elaborate and as implausibly disavowed as M.Vinteuil's display of his sheet music. Out for a walk, he has fallen asleep in the bushes mere centimeters from the living-room window, and upon awakening at dusk he remains hidden and watches the ensuing spectacle in the lighted interior of the house solely, he insists, out of fear of attracting attention and being suspected of wanting to watch. The narrator's "closetedness" in terms of his intention to spy is important to this scene, as is clear from Proust's various drafts: in an early version of this passage, voyeuristic motivation is clearly assumed, but the voyeur is the narrator's cousin; in the next version he himself is the voyeur, at which point voyeuristic intent is no longer admitted.[11]

The ritual between Mlle Vinteuil and her friend depends not only on the reiterated idea that M.Vinteuil is being made to witness the spectacle of his own profanation, but also on the notion that someone may be watching. This is in fact what enables the narrator to see the scene of

11. See Esquisses LI and LII, 1:796–805.

"sadism": he too is playing an implicit—and unwittingly complicit—role in their little drama. When Mlle Vinteuil coyly announces her intention of closing the shutters, her friend tells her to leave them open, and there ensues a discussion, evidently written into the script of their discursive foreplay, of the dangers and pleasures of being seen. The friend makes ironic comments about the likelihood of anyone seeing them at that hour in the middle of the countryside, and then concludes with "all the better that they should see us" (1:176; 1:159).

In other words, when the hero creates a clandestine theater for himself, he finds the stage occupied by actors in search of an audience. This scene of voyeurism, which sets the stage for the novel's presentation of Gomorrah, thus violates the very structure of voyeurism itself, which depends on an unsuspecting object.[12] Even if the two women being spied on at Montjouvain do not actually know that they are being watched, their pleasure centrally includes that possibility. It is thus they and not their voyeur who control the spectacle (the idea of control being another essential component of voyeurism),[13] as becomes clear when Mlle Vinteuil does finally close the shutters in the narrator's face before anything overtly sexual occurs; they are in charge of the curtain in their own drama.

The passage in which the narrator watches Charlus and Jupien's mutual discovery in the courtyard and then listens as they have sex, and the interlude in Jupien's brothel in which he observes Charlus chained to a bed, being whipped by a youth posing as a butcher's boy, are both clearly presented as spectacles. This is especially true of the brothel scene, which is as much a theatricalized ritual as Montjouvain. Nonetheless, and even despite the convenient transparency of the *oeil de boeuf* window through which the narrator watches Charlus's sadomasochistic tragicomedy, nei-

---

12. See Dorothy Kelly's interesting study of voyeurism in French literature, *Telling Glances* (New Brunswick, N.J.: Rutgers University Press, 1992), 7. Kelly's book contains a useful chapter on Proust (147–91), in which she discusses, among other aspects that will come into play in my own text, the reversibility of voyeurism whereby the watcher can become watched.

13. See Charles Rycroft, *A Critical Dictionary of Psychoanalysis* (London: Penguin, 1972), 194–95.

ther of these erotic spectacles depends for its eroticism on the idea of being seen.

Moreover, when the narrator witnesses scenes between men, nothing prevents him from following them to their logical conclusion. Even when he cannot actually see the lovemaking between Charlus and Jupien for logistical reasons, as I shall discuss presently, he is still able to understand what is going on. In contrast, at Montjouvain and in all subsequent attempts to understand what women do together, his comprehension is always blocked, and the curtain is always in some sense rung down prematurely.

Lest we imagine that exhibitionism is a taste peculiar to Mlle Vinteuil and her friend, one of the next glimpses we get of Gomorrah, in *Sodome et Gomorrhe II,* features two lesbians deliberately creating a scandal at the Grand-Hôtel in Balbec: "Bloch's sister had for some time past been indulging, with a retired actress, in secret relations which presently ceased to suffice them. They felt that to be seen would add perversity to their pleasure, and chose to flaunt their dangerous embraces before the eyes of all the world" (2:871; 3:236). Hotel patrons complain about the women's increasingly ostentatious behavior, and grave consequences are averted only because of the protection of M. Nissim Bernard, Mlle Bloch's uncle and himself a comical figure of the Sodomite. A few days later the young women are at it again, to the horrified fascination of onlookers, and to the narrator's distress as he worries about Albertine (2:879; 3:244).

Lesbian relations alone are apparently not deviant enough for the likes of Mlles Vinteuil and Bloch and their respective girlfriends: being seen adds perversity to their pleasure. Again, it is important to note that the exhibitionism shown to be a standard feature of Gomorrhean sexuality does not appear in the novel's repertoire of Sodomite perversions. Charlus may enjoy being tied up and whipped, but neither he nor others any of his ilk ever seek to parade their relations in public (except in the covert form of strictly third-person observations). To the contrary, the narrator's repeated inadvertent stumblings on scenes between men notwithstanding, the men in question try, however ineptly at times, to keep such practices under wraps and maintain the illusion of heterosexuality. M. Nissim Bernard, for example, in sharp contrast to his niece, is the soul of (at least attempted) discretion: while energetically pursuing servant boys, he is described as "endeavoring at the same time to escape notice and to avoid a scandal" (2:874; 3:239).[14] Perhaps most remarkably, when Charlus tries to catch Morel cheating on him—with a mysterious seducer who turns out, unbeknownst to the baron, to be his own cousin—Morel gets wind of the plan and presents only an eerie spectacle of stilted heterosexuality (2:112–18; 3:463–68).

The depiction of lesbians as flamboyantly exhibitionistic and male homosexuals as scrupulously discreet is paradoxical. For one thing, of course, it contradicts more recent notions of "lesbian invisibility" versus gay male ostentation; but then, as we have seen, lesbians were a much more visible presence than male "inverts" in French literature at the time Proust was writing.[15] Within the novel, lesbian self-advertisement is remarkable, especially because Gomorrah, as opposed to the increasingly visible Sodom, comes to figure precisely that which cannot be seen. Throughout the later volumes of the novel, the narrator spends a great deal of time trying to observe what women do together, and his efforts are always unsuccessful. Gomorrhean sexuality thus presents the peculiar paradox of being at once exhibitionistic and yet impossible actually to see. Proust invests in Gomorrah not just an erotics of sameness, as we saw in Chapter 2, but also the novel's sole model of a sexuality in control of itself, or at least of its own representation. This is, as Sedgwick so conclusively demonstrates, precisely what Sodom is not: "If Charlus's being in the closet means that he possesses a secret knowledge, it means all the more that everyone around him does; their incessant reading of the plot of his preserving his secret from them provides an all the more eventful plot for them to keep secret from him" (225–26).

Gomorrah would seem to escape this fate precisely by parading itself in full view. Because they call attention to their scandalous presence, women such as Bloch's sister and cousin and Léa avoid the "glass closet" in which

14. For a remarkable analysis of the importance of M. Nissim Bernard as a model of "avuncularity" in the novel, see Richard Goodkin, *Around Proust* (Princeton: Princeton University Press, 1991), chap. 1.

15. On the paucity of lesbian representation in recent French literature, see Anne F. Garréta, "In Light of Invisibility," *Yale French Studies* 90 (1996), 205–13.

Charlus becomes trapped. Because Charlus hides his predilections, every-one not only knows about them but is further able to enjoy the spectacle of his believing himself to be hiding. By the same token, then, the women who disport themselves in public manage to do what is otherwise impossible: to control what is known about their sexuality.[16] If the couple at Montjouvain had not been excited by the prospect of being seen, the narrator would never have seen them, nor would his jealousy be inflamed at the thought that Albertine may know Mlle Vinteuil, Léa, or Bloch's cousin if those women had not decided to parade their private affairs in the public realm. Gomorrah would be entirely invisible in the novel if it did not deliberately display itself.

Albertine's Desires

The character in the *Recherche* who most obviously and completely em-bodies control over other people's knowledge of her sexuality is Alber-tine, who eludes definition throughout the book. As Margaret Gray points out, critics have tended to imitate the narrator's quest for an answer to the question posed by her desires by insisting that a solution can be located in the text if one looks hard enough, or at the right edition.[17]

Kaja Silverman, whose final chapter in *Male Subjectivity at the Margins* offers one of the most nuanced readings of Proustian sexuality, takes an

16. Heterosexuality is hardly less prone to transparency than Sodom in the *Recherche*. For instance, however much Swann and the narrator may lie in order to manipulate their mis-tresses, their efforts are never successful in fooling anyone. Gomorrah seems to be the sole exception to the Proustian axiom, similar to psychoanalytic doctrine, that the truth, particu-larly the sexual truth, will always out.

17. She notes, for instance, that some critics have demonstrated greater credulity than the narrator himself in their zeal to resolve Albertine's mystery and thus "domesticate Gomor-rah." See the chapter titled "Marcel's 'Ecriture Feminine'" in Margaret Gray's useful and en-tertaining *Postmodern Proust* (Philadelphia: University of Pennsylvania Press, 1992), 94–114; quotation 101. I am assuming throughout, as Gray argues, but as many critics have not, that Albertine is essentially characterized by unknowability, and that the publication of Grasset's alternative text of *Albertine disparue* (*La Fugitive*) in 1987, which places Albertine's death near Montjouvain, does not offer a definitive solution to the mystery of her sexuality.

idiosyncratic approach to the question of the ultimate meaning of Albertine by suggesting that lesbianism represents the "truth" not merely of her sexuality but of the narrator's as well. "Why not think of Marcel simply as a lesbian?" she asks, adding that his "character is established as being psychically female, but corporeally male, and hence 'a woman's soul enclosed in a man's body.' "[18] I entirely agree with Silverman's argument that what must be emphasized in Proust's depiction of female sexuality is "the refusal to project castration onto the corporeality of the sexual Other, and thereby to secure the phallus as the unquestioned signifier of power, privilege, and wholeness" (388). Nonetheless, it seems to me that there are good reasons for not "think[ing] of Marcel simply as a lesbian."[19]

For a start, as Silverman herself amply demonstrates, nothing having to do with the nexus of gender and sexual preference in Proust's novel is simple.[20] Not only does the narrator not depict himself as conforming to Ulrichs's formula, but also the problem he repeatedly encounters in trying to understand Albertine's sexuality is that he is neither corporeally nor psychically female; he does not resemble her. As Leo Bersani puts it, "Albertine's lesbianism represents a nearly inconceivable yet inescapable identity of sameness and otherness in Marcel's desires; lesbianism is a relation of sameness which Marcel is condemned to see as an irreducibly unknowable otherness."[21] It is this opaque alterity of Albertine's desire for her like that fuels the intrigue of *La Prisonnière* and *Albertine disparue,* and that makes it problematic to try to think either of Albertine as Albert or of the narrator as a lesbian.

Several scenes make it clear that, even if he would indeed like to be able to think of himself as a lesbian, his gender presents an insurmount-

18. Kaja Silverman, *Male Subjectivity at the Margins* (New York: Routledge, 1992), 386; subsequently cited in the text.

19. Emma Wilson also takes issue with Silverman's formulation in her chapter on Proust in *Sexuality and the Reading Process* (Oxford: Oxford University Press, 1996), 71–94. Wilson's readings parallel my own in several particulars.

20. I discuss Silverman's reading of Proustian sexuality more fully in Chapter 5.

21. Leo Bersani, " 'The Culture of Redemption': Marcel Proust and Melanie Klein," in *Critical Inquiry* 12, no. 2 (Winter 1986), 416.

able obstacle. Twice after Albertine's death he imagines that he has found what he is looking for, but both impressions turn out to be deceptive. In the first, while talking with Andrée, the narrator suddenly perceives her as a living template of Albertine's desires: "For the first time she seemed to me beautiful. I said to myself that her almost frizzy hair, her dark, shadowed eyes, were doubtless what Albertine had loved so much, the materialisation before my eyes of what she pictured in her amorous day-dreams" (3:556; 4:126).

Identifying with what he imagines to have been Albertine's desire for Andrée, he vicariously sees her as a sexual object. He adds, "I seemed to see before me, the unlooked-for exhumation of a priceless relic, the incarnate desire of Albertine which Andrée was to me, as Venus was the desire of Jove" (3:557; 4:127). He interrogates Andrée about her past with Albertine, and, to his surprise, she readily admits that she herself likes women, but maintains that her friend did not. She also refuses his entreaties to allow him to watch as she demonstrates even the most rudimentary caresses with one of her friends. He realizes, from her flustered response to a question, that he will never get the truth from Andrée: "I sensed that whatever I saw from now on would have been artificially arranged for my benefit" (3:557; 4:127). This is no mere momentary contingency, of course, but the only condition under which he ever sees what goes on between women.

At this point, though, something untoward occurs: whereas in Andrée he had previously perceived only an allegorical figure of Albertine's desire, he now sees his own image reflected in her face: "At that moment I caught sight of myself in the mirror, and was struck by a certain resemblance between myself and Andrée. If I had not long since ceased to shave my upper lip and had had only a faint shadow of a moustache, this resemblance would have been almost complete" (3:559; 4:129).

The resemblance the narrator suddenly finds between Andrée and himself should perhaps be read as an echo of the rivalry between brother and sister over the same woman in Balzac's *Fille aux yeux d'or*.[22] He has al-

---

22. Anne Chevalier discusses implicit references to this work in the novel in her "Notice" to *Albertine disparue* (although she does not mention this scene); see 4:1022.

ready, in *À l'ombre des jeunes filles en fleurs,* remarked that she reminds him of himself. In fact, this is what had prevented him from being attracted to her: "Andrée was too intellectual, too neurotic, too sickly, too like myself for me really to love her" (1:1005; 2:295). If Andrée is at once the incarnation of Albertine's desire and a female version of himself, though, he should perhaps no longer feel himself categorically excluded by that desire. As in the Balzac story, Albertine might be expected to have fallen for the male version of her female lover. And yet here it is the narrator who functions as a pale imitation of his female counterpart: he conjectures that it was his resemblance to Andrée, before his mustache grew in, that led Albertine to leave him in Balbec to rejoin her friend in Paris. The resemblance between them, he suggests, works to Andrée's advantage, not his.

The idea that his maleness is what prevents him from even conceptually possessing Albertine leads him to give up identifying with her object of desire and attempt instead to identify with her as subject. His sexual obsession has by this time been completely taken over by the epistemological force that drives all Proustian desire: "I was happier at having Andrée in my company than I would have been at having an Albertine miraculously restored to life. For Andrée could tell me more things about Albertine than Albertine herself had ever told me" (3:612; 4:180). When Andrée ceases to deny her friend's taste for other women and instead alludes to Albertine's "furious desire" for such pleasures, the narrator can think only of attempting to insert himself into the picture in Albertine's place: "The idea that a woman had perhaps had relations with Albertine no longer aroused in me anything save the desire to have relations with that woman myself" (3:612; 4:180). Andrée, catching his drift, replies that it would be impossible to reproduce their lovemaking heterosexually: "Ah! yes, but you're a man. And so we can't do quite the same things as I used to do with Albertine" (3:612; 4:179).

This inaccessible alterity of feminine pleasure, and the ultimate invisibility of sexual relations between women, are dramatized in especially noteworthy manner in the second scene in which the narrator has a false impression of understanding Albertine's sexuality. In his desire to see some simulacrum of Albertine's pleasure, he hires two laundresses to make love to each other in a brothel. This passage is remarkable in that, although the situation would seem to offer a sort of corrective to the Montjouvain episode—having hired the actors, he now controls the drama—and although he is now able to witness an actual sex scene, that scene nevertheless remains invisible. Despite having arranged for it to be played out in front of him, he cannot see it: the passage contains no visual description at all. The narrator conveys only what he can hear, and the sound made by one of the women under the caresses of the other is recognizable to him only by an effort of his imagination. "It took me some time," he says, "to understand that this noise expressed what, by analogy with the (very different) sensations I myself had felt, I called pleasure" (3:561; 4:131).

Once again, as Freud puts it, things between the sexes "must be similar, though in some way or other they must nevertheless be different." Confronted with the spectacle of that difference, the narrator seizes on its audible manifestation in order to force it into an analogy that only emphasizes its unrecognizability. He says nothing about what he sees, and we can only conclude that he sees nothing.

The narrator's apparent blindness to the scene between the two laundresses has a certain precedent in the passage in which he witnesses Charlus and Jupien having sex in the latter's tailor shop. There, too, the description is purely auditory, but a reason is given: the narrator, hidden in the empty shop next door, is logistically unable to watch the proceedings without revealing his presence, and so he must be content with listening. While the two scenes have much in common because of their shared auditory description, I would argue that they are distinct in both conception and effect.

For one thing, the move from the visual presentation of the seduction of Charlus and Jupien to the auditory presentation of their lovemaking may well have taken its motivation from the author's desire to escape censorship: he could not have included a visually explicit description of penetrative sex between men. (The only fully visible scene of a sexual act in the entire *Recherche* is at once the most conceptually shocking and the least genitally oriented: Charlus's flagellation in the brothel, which also occurs toward the end of the novel; published after the author's death, and after his readers had already accepted the other passages, this scene was less likely to attract opprobrium.) But the French reading public had already, as I discussed in Chapter 2, been exposed to scenes between women, and even if such representations retained their capacity to shock, the public had become somewhat inured to them, which was not the case for male homosexual scenes. The absence of visual description therefore seems more comprehensible, in practical terms, in the Charlus-Jupien scene than in the episode of the two laundresses.

For whatever extratextual reasons, Proust's narrator hears rather than sees both scenes, and the Baudelairean theme of resemblance between pleasure and pain, lovemaking and violence, is invoked in both passages. The central difference is that what he overhears coming from Jupien's shop is ultimately comprehensible to him, even if disconcerting. There the violent implications of the sounds are attenuated by the somewhat comical manner in which they are described:

> It is true that these sounds were so violent that, if they had not always been taken up an octave higher by a parallel plaint, I might have thought that one person was slitting another's throat within a few feet of me, and that subsequently the murderer and his resuscitated victim were taking a bath to wash away the traces of the crime. I concluded from this later on that there is another thing as vociferous as pain, namely pleasure, especially when there is added to it . . . an immediate concern about cleanliness. (2:631; 3:11)

The pleasures of Sodom may sound like murderous violence, but it is of the sort seen in cartoons, in which characters routinely get blown to bits or flattened by steamrollers only to reappear, hardly the worse for wear. Despite (or perhaps because of) the penetrative violence in the encounter between the two men, clearly suggested in the last sentence of this passage, it is described in terms that imply a qualitatively lesser strangeness than Gomorrhean pleasure. Sodom, even when not staged, offers stage violence, the familiar catharsis of Roadrunner and Coyote. Since Proust had no access to Warner Brothers cartoons, of course, it might be more apt to invoke a similar phenomenon in French literature: the fate of Sade's heroines, notably Justine and Juliette, who are subjected to endless and varied mistreatment, endlessly to emerge unscathed.

What goes on between the two laundresses, although it has been staged expressly so that the narrator can see what women do together, is neither visible nor auditorily domesticated, as is the scene between

Charlus and Jupien. All the narrator is able to grasp from the sounds of the laundress's pleasure is its intensity, along with its utter alterity: this pleasure, he says, "must have been very great to overwhelm to this extent the person who was expressing it and to extract from her this strange utterance [*ce langage inconnu*] (3:561; 4:131). Despite the Baudelairean overtones of the narrator's commentary, we are far from the depiction in "Delphine et Hippolyte" that posits lesbian pleasure as tacit and recognizable, "the silent hymn that pleasure sings."[23] Remarkably, the narrator never questions the authenticity of the scene, which is essentially a private theatrical production in a brothel, and which he therefore knows to have been "artificially arranged for his benefit," as he puts it in reference to Andrée. All that he concludes is what he already suspects: Gomorrah has its own incomprehensible language of pleasure, which means that Gomorrhean pleasure is essentially different from anything he can imagine.

The purely auditory nature of the description reinforces the narrator's alienation from the brothel scene, but not the scene in the tailor shop.[24] From the sounds made by Charlus and Jupien, strange and violent though they initially seem, the narrator extrapolates what might have been a horrifying scenario, rendered innocuous by its essential masculine comprehensibility. In contrast, the "exquisite drama which the young woman was living through" (again, he does not consider the fact that it is a drama she is staging for his benefit) remains invisible. It is hidden from his eyes, he says, by "the curtain that is forever lowered for other people over what happens in the mysterious intimacy of every human creature" (3:561; 4:131). The shutters that Mlle Vinteuil closes in his face in the Montjouvain scene thus find their precise metaphoric equivalent here, but the curtain that comes down in this passage is presented under the misleading

23. "Le cantique muet que chante le plaisir." Baudelaire, *Oeuvres complètes,* 1:153.
24. The alienating effect of a voice removed from its visual context is a theme Proust treats a number of times, always in terms of women's voices, and often, for obvious reasons, in the context of telephone conversations. This is particularly dramatic in the scene in *Le Côté de Guermantes I* in which the grandmother's voice on the telephone prefigures her death: "This isolation of the voice was like a symbol, an evocation, a direct consequence of another isolation" (2:136; 2:433).

auspices of a generalized alterity that masks the particular invisibility of feminine pleasure: "the palpitating specificity of feminine pleasure," as he puts it shortly before this passage (3:538; 4:108).

Albertine's Sex

The depiction of Gomorrhean sexuality as at once exhibitionistic and invisible is reflected in anatomical terms in the novel's sole description of the female body. The portrait of Albertine's nude body in *La Prisonnière* has been repeatedly cited by critics in order to prove various critical points. In particular, it has been the focus of attempts to determine whether Albertine is "really" a man. Let us take a fresh look at the passage in question:

> Before Albertine obeyed and took off her shoes, I would open her chemise. Her two little uplifted breasts were so round that they seemed not so much to be an integral part of her body as to have ripened there like fruit; and her belly (concealing the place where a man's is disfigured as though by an iron clamp left sticking in a statue that has been taken down from its niche) was closed, at the junction of her thighs, by two valves with a curve as languid, as reposeful, as cloistral as that of the horizon after the sun has set. She would take off her shoes, and lie down by my side. (3:74; 3:587)

One aspect of this passage that critics tend to leave out is its frame: I have reproduced here the entire paragraph, whereas it is invariably quoted minus its opening and closing sentences. What these elements foreground is Albertine's willing availability to the narrator. The description is suspended in the moment between his demand and her compliance. He is able to contemplate her body not, as in a famous scene immediately preceding this one, while she is asleep and thus with only unwitting consent on her part, but because she allows him to. Again, the view of female sexuality—specifically, in this scene, of the female sex—that the narrator sees is one that is controlled by the woman in question. (This is why his most perfect moment with her is when she is asleep: it is the only time he does not need her permission, and he is able to "possess" her in the absence of any trace of her subjectivity, her own desire.)

What he finds when he looks at Albertine's body is haunted, as J. E. Rivers points out, by what he does not find: male genitalia. This should not, however, lead us, as it does Rivers, to conclude that "the whole description has a distinct flavor of protesting too much," and thus that the passage, "when viewed from a slightly tilted angle, take[s] on a distinctly homosexual coloration." [25] Instead, it must be emphasized that the narrator's parenthetical reference to what is not there privileges what is. As Silverman observes, "this passage marks the *male* rather than the *female* body negatively, and precisely at that site whose conventional valorization facilitates a masculine identification with the phallus" (379).

The narrator sees in Albertine's body its difference from the male body, its difference from his own. The fact that he cannot really discern what lies between her thighs does not necessarily suggest a conventional representation, à la Freud, of woman as defined by the lack of an essential component. Rather, in the context of a work in which the protagonist's most ardent and futile desire is to see female sexuality in action, it functions as an anatomical enactment of the novel's central erotic predicament. She is there, in front of him, willing to take off everything, and yet he still cannot see what defines her. [26]

Through the Looking Glass

In contrast to the narrator's always fruitless attempts to see what remains invisible to him, Gomorrhean sexuality itself privileges the visual, and not only in terms of the exhibitionistic bent displayed by various characters. [27] Most strikingly, in the passages in *Sodome et Gomorrhe* in which the narrator suddenly becomes aware of meaningful glances exchanged between

25. Rivers, *Proust and the Art of Love*, 213.

26. As Dorothy Kelly notes in discussing this passage, "The woman in this scene is not completely exposed; a man's gaze cannot unveil just what a woman is" (*Telling Glances*, 175).

27. See Kelly's discussion of the relation between the narrator's gaze and Albertine's, ibid., esp. 176–77.

attractive young women all around him, lesbian desire is frequently described as a luminescent emanation: "Often, in the hall of the Casino, when two girls were smitten with mutual desire, a sort of luminous phenomenon occurred, as it were a phosphorescent trail flashing from one to the other" (2:880–81; 3:245).

Just after the scandal at the Grand-Hôtel in Balbec caused by Léa and Mlle Bloch, a woman appears on the beach who further excites the narrator's anxieties. This woman figures as a sort of embodiment of Gomorrah, which means that she is all eyes: "I had noticed on the beach a handsome young woman, slender and pale, whose eyes, round their center, scattered rays so geometrically luminous that one was reminded, on meeting her gaze, of some constellation." She immediately, of course, begins making eyes at Albertine: "I saw that she never ceased to fasten upon Albertine the alternating and revolving beam of her gaze" (2:879–80; 3:245). Metaphors of luminosity accumulate as the narrator watches this form of overtly covert communication as though it were some sort of celestial Morse code. Before long, this human lighthouse sees Bloch's cousin for the first time, and the two have soon fooled the woman's oblivious husband into thinking that they are childhood friends, despite the fact that she does not know her "old friend's" name (2:881; 3:246).

Silly as this scene may be, it underscores the point that Gomorrheans do not seem to need names, or even words, to communicate with one another. Their intimacy is immediate, and it takes place in a realm of wordless sensuality beyond the comprehension of witnesses to their phosphorescent assignations. The narrator's repeated insistence on using light imagery to describe how these women make contact sets their relations apart from the more pedestrian Masonic signals exchanged between denizens of Sodom, and demonstrates the centrality of vision that is peculiar to Gomorrhean eroticism.

The centerpiece of Gomorrhean optics is, unsurprisingly, the looking glass. It is no accident that one of the first real hints the narrator gets of Albertine's "secret life" comes to light through a mirror. Some fifty pages before the scenes I have been discussing, he is in the ballroom at the Balbec casino with Albertine and Andrée when the demoiselles Bloch enter. The narrator and his companions all self-consciously ignore the newcomers: he refuses to acknowledge them because of their sapphic reputation (and despite the fact that they "had both turned out extremely pretty"); Andrée notes that she and Albertine are horrified by such creatures; Albertine herself turns her back on them. Despite her ostentatious snubbing of the "disreputable pair," the narrator sees a look of "deep attentiveness" momentarily come into Albertine's eyes. His disquiet increases when she insists too vehemently that she did not notice the women at all. She finally gives herself away in response to his remark (one of his few successful lies) that the women had not looked at them either. She replies, hotly, that in fact the demoiselles Bloch had done nothing but stare at them the entire time they were in the ballroom. At this point, in the face of his puzzlement, she is forced to divulge the means by which she has been able to watch a scene taking place behind her back: "a large mirror which I had not noticed and upon which I now realised that my friend, while talking to me, had never ceased to fix her beautiful preoccupied eyes" (2:830–31; 3:197–98).

Albertine's ruse here improbably recalls the opening scene in *The Hound of the Baskervilles,* in which Sherlock Holmes amazes Watson by his ability to see what is going on behind him, and in response to the latter's astonishment replies that he does not have eyes in the back of his head but rather a polished silver coffeepot in front of him. I have dwelt on this casino scene in some detail because it is emblematic of the way Gomorrah functions in the *Recherche.* While Albertine appears to be paying attention to the narrator, her gaze is actually fixated on a mirror image which he cannot discern. His desire, and the nature of female relations, endow her in this context with the acuity of a Sherlock Holmes and himself with the dull-wittedness of a Watson. There seems to exist a looking-glass world of Gomorrhean relations that he cannot understand beyond the extent to which it is displayed to him, just as Watson's powers of detection, despite his enormous efforts, extend only to what Holmes deigns to point out to him.[28]

---

28. Sir Arthur Conan Doyle, *The Complete Sherlock Holmes,* 2 vols. (New York: Bantam, 1986), 2:3. The invocation of Sherlock Holmes in a discussion of Proust would seem to be perfectly in keeping with the narrator's semiotic fervor; what is noteworthy about this moment is that it turns Albertine into Holmes and the narrator into Watson, with whom he shares the narrative function, but in principle, if not in practice, little else.

The narrator is unable to perceive Gomorrah, except by its negative contours, which he provokes Albertine into explaining to him. It is, moreover, her very narcissism that causes her to reveal her momentary secret: perfectly willing to insist that she does not see the other women, she is unable to remain silent at the suggestion that they do not see her.[29] Until he manages to exploit this weakness, and thus gain a fleeting glimpse of how this world operates, the narrator must be content with the reflection of a reflection, seeing only the passing change of expression in Albertine's eyes as she watches the women watching her.

As I have suggested, Gomorrah is the only example in the novel of a sexuality in control of itself and able to play with, rather than be played by, the image it projects. Lesbian sexuality thus escapes the dynamics of the closet which present Sodom as an unwitting spectacle. Instead, as at Montjouvain, it is the viewer who is forced into a voyeuristic "closet." Far from representing a trivial distraction that must be pushed aside before the narrator can muster the self-discipline needed to transcend the realm of contingent sexuality, Gomorrah embodies precisely what he is unable to attain: a coincidence of desire and fulfillment that finds realization elsewhere only in the novel's deferred Ouroboros structure. In the chapters that follow, we shall see how the development of Proust's depiction of lesbianism comes to incorporate this impossible fantasy.

29. Here, of course, my Sherlock Holmes analogy crumbles, as the great detective displays no such Achilles' heel of vanity.

4

The Evolution of Gomorrah

In the previous chapters I have argued that the standard Proust-inspired reading of Gomorrah as a mere counterpart to or transposition of Sodom constitutes an error, one that does an unfortunate disservice to the nuanced depiction of sexuality in the *Recherche*. Gomorrah did not, however, spring fully formed from the author's brow, and in Proust's earlier works lesbianism functions in something very much like the manner that has misleadingly been attributed to it in the novel. In this chapter I trace the evolution of Proust's portrayal of female homosexuality, first demonstrating that in his pre-*Recherche* writings of the 1890s, lesbianism does duty for male homosexuality. The meaning of same-sex desire between women changes in the course of his work from a relatively transparent displacement of what would later become Sodom to the enigmatic polysexuality of Albertine, and even of Morel as he crosses over into an inexplicable "lesbianism." Along the way, several points may be discerned at which different stages of Proust's depiction of relations between women come together, in particular, in a scene from the early unfinished novel *Jean Santeuil,* and in the portrait of Mlle Vinteuil in "Combray." After discussing Proust's earlier portrayals of lesbianism, I will examine the scenes in *La Prisonnière* in which Gomorrah most clearly represents the unpredictable excessiveness of female sexuality.

During the 1890s Proust was far from being perceived as the illustrious author of serious works. On the contrary, he was known, to the extent that he was known at all, as a somewhat ridiculous young dilettante who had, largely as a result of his social connections, published an overpriced volume of short stories and poems for which he managed to secure a preface by Anatole France and illustrations by the society hostess and floral painter Madeleine Lemaire. *Les Plaisirs et les jours* (Pleasures and Days), as he called it after a work of Hesiod, *Les Travaux et les jours* in French (Works and Days), appeared in 1896, composed almost entirely of pieces that had previously been published in literary magazines.

Despite their decadent and sometimes homoerotic tone, male homosexuality is not mentioned as such in any of Proust's writings from this era, during which he tended to approach delicate subjects from a female viewpoint. Lesbianism figures in several pieces in a way that is clearly intended to represent homosexuality "in general," while in another it is female heterosexuality that serves as a shameful secret. Three of the stories from the period of *Les Plaisirs et les jours* are especially germane to my argument: "Violante ou la mondanité" ("Violante, or Wordly Vanities"), "la Confession d'une jeune fille" (A Young Girl's Confession), and "Avant la nuit" (Before Nightfall).[1]

"Violante ou la mondanité"

"Violante ou la mondanité," written in 1892, when Proust was twenty-one, is one of his earliest published works. It first appeared in *Le Banquet* before being reprinted in *Les Plaisirs et les jours.* As its title suggests, "Violante" is a satirical treatment of the theme to which Proust was to return repeatedly, that of the dangers of succumbing to the lure of high society.

1. These stories are all collected in Marcel Proust, *Pleasures and Days,* ed. F. W. Dupee, trans. Louise Varèse, Gerard Hopkins, and Barbara Dupee (New York: Howard Fertig, 1978). All references in the text are to this edition, followed by the page reference to the Pléiade edition, *Jean Santeuil, précédé de Les Plaisirs et les jours,* ed. Pierre Clarac and Yves Sandre (Paris: Gallimard, 1971).

The heroine's trajectory in this moral tale à la Voltaire is evident from its chapter headings: from the purity of her "meditative childhood" Violante is initiated into a vaguely defined yet clearly pernicious "sensuality" by a sixteen-year-old boy, feels the "pangs of love," and then irrevocably loses her native innocence to "worldly vanities."

Homosexuality puts in its first appearance per se in Proust's fictional work in "Violante," in the form of a woman who incarnates the immorality of high society. In the last section of the story, when Violante has already begun her descent into wordly corruption, she is accosted—indeed, sexually harassed—by this woman, the princesse de Misène, who claims to be a friend of her mother. She flees this most dreadful representative of societal immorality, who, lest we have missed the point, is subsequently identified as having a keen appreciation for feminine beauty. Violante eventually dies without having extricated herself from her elegant plight, but she remains impervious to this particular form of worldly danger.

This first mention of lesbianism in Proust's writing, associated with the immorality of *le monde,* anticipates one of the functions of male homosexuality in the *Recherche:* the princesse de Misène reads as a very primitive version of Charlus in his role as would-be seducer of the narrator under the guise of mentor. Female homoeroticism is also linked to the maternal role, in that the pretext offered by the princesse de Misène for her caresses is that she was close to Violante's mother and had once held the heroine on her lap. Mother-daughter eroticism is, as we shall see in the next chapter, the hidden cornerstone of Gomorrah in the *Recherche.* Another important aspect of the maternal role in Proust's writing also comes to light in "Violante," and it is, moreover, one that has great importance both in these early texts and throughout his work: maternal profanation and matricide, specifically in the form of the child's sexuality somehow causing the mother's death.

In "Violante" this theme is at once well hidden in the plot and inscribed in the name of its eponymous heroine. Her peculiar name justifies itself implicitly on the first page, where we are told that her sole character flaw, like that of many a Proustian protagonist, is a lack of willpower (*manque de volonté*): "This lack of will power inspired in Violante's mother fears that might with time have borne fruit if the viscountess with her husband had not, while out hunting one day, met with a violent end [*péri violemment*], leaving Violante an orphan at fifteen" (25; 29). Thus we find, in the form of a strategically placed adverb, the first occurrence of matricide in Proust's writing: Violante's lack of will is itself her violence, which causes her mother's death. The latter dies "violently," which is to say at the grammatical hands of her daughter. Her untimely demise thus spares her the years of worry that become the lot of the narrator's mother and grandmother in the *Recherche*.[2]

"La Confession d'une jeune fille"

The theme of matricide finds its most hyperbolic fictional realization in "La Confession d'une jeune fille," a story published for the first time in *Les Plaisirs et les jours*.[3] "Confession" tells essentially the same story as "Violante," except that here the focus is no longer centrally on *mondanité*, and the matricide hidden in the first paragraph of the earlier piece takes quite explicit form, indeed, is the point of the story. "Confession" consists of the first-person narrative of a young woman who has shot herself out of guilt over causing her mother's death; she tells her story before succumbing to her wounds. As in the previous story, the heroine has wasted her life in frivolous worldly pursuits following her erotic initiation by a young male cousin. (In "Violante" the corruptor is a sixteen-year-old friend of her young aunt, while in the *Recherche* the narrator mentions in passing having lost his virginity to a cousin; the theme of the initiating cousin is one that reappears often in Proust's work.)

The narrator's fatal flaw in "Confession" is also the same as in "Violante": "What grieved my mother was my lack of will" (83; 89). Here,

2. The narrator of the *Recherche* also blames his lack of willpower for the death of his grandmother and the eventual death of his mother as well. Ghislain de Diesbach interprets Violante's name differently: "Despite her name, Violante is anything but violent and seems on the contrary born to be violated [En dépit de son prénom, Violante n'a rien de violent et semble plutôt faite pour être violée]." Ghislain de Diesbach, *Proust* (Paris: Perrin, 1991), 135.

3. Proust later returned to the subject of matricide in a remarkable essay titled "Sentiments filiaux d'un parricide" (Filial Sentiments of a Parricide), discussed in the next chapter.

involuntary matricide is the explicit result of the *manque de volonté* that both female protagonists share with Jean Santeuil and the narrator of the *Recherche*. Throughout Proust's writing this failure of will is linked to a neglect of what is posited as truly important in life—art, nature, solitary contemplation—in favor of the frivolous attractions of society, but "Confession" makes it plain that what is centrally at stake is sexuality. The narrator of "Confession" kills her mother in a manner that clearly anticipates M. Vinteuil's death as a result of his daughter's sexual excesses. The voyeuristic role that is posthumously forced on M. Vinteuil's portrait in the Montjouvain scene can also be found here: in "Confession" the mother dies from witnessing her daughter's sexuality. Her fragile system—she has a weak heart to match her delicate sensibility—succumbs to the shocking sight of her daughter in the embrace of a young man.

The scandal of what the mother witnesses does not arise out of the fact that the man is not her daughter's fiancé; the heroine's infidelity to her intended is merely a symptom of her uncontrollable lust. What kills the mother is the look of bestial sensuality on her daughter's face, the spectacle of her desire itself. The narrator refers to her sexuality—her *hetero*sexuality—as "the secret crime of my life" (86; 92). This disproportionate characterization of the normal as deviant, along with the idea that the mother could die of horror merely by catching sight of her daughter's lust-filled visage, suggests that something more than hyperbolic prudery is at stake in this story. One need not be an inveterate proponent of biographical criticism to read "Confession" in the light of homosexual guilt. Should any doubt remain as to the nature of the otherwise incomprehensible "secret crime" being recounted here, Proust's addition of an epigraph from the final, condemnatory section of "Delphine et Hippolyte" serves to dispel it (84; 90). In this early story, female heterosexual desire, linked to lesbianism through the Baudelaire quotation, is an apparent stand-in for male homosexuality. Moreover, "Confession," which Proust dedicated to Robert de Montesquiou (legendarily one of the models for Charlus), seems to be a reworking of an earlier story, "Avant la nuit," which deals with similar themes, but in a somewhat less veiled manner, using the more coherent "secret crime" of lesbianism rather than female heterosexuality.

"Avant la nuit"

"Avant la nuit" ("Before Nightfall"), which had been published in *La Revue blanche* in 1893, was omitted from *Les Plaisirs et les jours* and replaced by "Confession." This story also takes the form of the sexual confession of a woman who has shot herself and, again like a moribund soprano in nineteenth-century opera, delivers her tale while waiting to expire. It is possible that "Avant la nuit" was excluded from *Les Plaisirs* because Proust preferred "Confession" for aesthetic reasons, or perhaps he feared repercussions from the earlier story's more obviously risqué subject matter. It seems likely that he wished to avoid appearing preoccupied with defending homosexuality of any stripe; after all, *Chansons de Bilitis* and other works of the same period managed to avoid implicating their authors by portraying lesbianism lasciviously rather than sympathetically, and "Avant la nuit" is anything but lascivious. (A translation of "Avant la nuit" appeared in 1960 in *The Ladder,* the publication of the Daughters of Bilitis, presumably for this very reason.)[4] In any case, the close structural resemblance between this story and "Confession" emphasizes what is already evident: Proust kept exploring the same theme of sexual guilt, trying out various means of expressing through female characters the subject he would not deal with directly.

"Avant la nuit" is essentially an apologia for homosexuality. Although the suicidal protagonist is a woman, the piece is not about lesbianism per se. The story both overtly and implicitly establishes an equivalence between male and female homosexuality which sets it apart from the depiction of Gomorrah in the *Recherche.* Unlike the young woman in "Confession d'une jeune fille," the confessional heroine in "Avant la nuit" has a name and an interlocutor. Françoise, the main character, recounts her guilty secret to Leslie, her heterosexual male friend, whose narrative frames the story. In the course of confessing her secret to Leslie, she reminds him of his own earlier speech justifying homosexuality on the occasion of another woman's having been caught with a female lover. Among his arguments had been the following statement, which makes it

---

4. See Marcel Proust, "In the Twilight," trans. Abigail Sanford, *The Ladder* 5 (1960), 4–8.

clear that what is at issue is not lesbianism itself: "How can we be shocked by practices of which Socrates (it was a question of men, but it's the same thing, isn't it?), who drank the hemlock rather than commit an injustice, heartily approved among his favorite friends?"[5]

It is not by chance that the task of defending homosexuality is assigned to a character who is absolved of any but the most rigorously intellectual interest in the subject. Leslie declares himself personally disturbed, as is customary among first-person Proustian narrators, by what he defends in principle.[6] The only specifically female trait lent to Françoise is that Leslie regards her as a mother figure (a trait shared by the repellent princesse de Misène in "Violante"). In all other respects, the justification of homosexuality in "Avant la nuit" is an early variant of what later became the essay on inversion referred to as "La Race des Tantes." Numerous elements of the argument anticipate passages from that section of *Sodome et Gomorrhe I*. In both Françoise's explanation of how her tendencies came to manifest themselves in her life and in the account of male homosexuality in the *Recherche*, for instance, we find a discussion of the influence of knowledge and aesthetics on natural inclinations of attraction and disgust, and in both cases a key reference is to Michelet's observations about jellyfish. The lesbian narrator of "Avant la nuit," overtly implicated in the discussion of deviance, couches the jellyfish comparison in objective terms: "In the truly artistic nature physical attraction or repulsion is qualified by the contemplation of the beautiful. Most people turn away from the jellyfish in disgust. Michelet, who appreciated the delicacy of their colors, collected them with pleasure" (270; 170). The narrator of the *Recherche*, doubtless to emphasize his own innate aversion to such things as jellyfish and homosexuality, makes this same allusion in personal terms: "When I followed my

---

5. "Avant la Nuit," translated by J. E. Rivers, appears as an appendix to *Proust and the Art of Love*, 267–71; quotation 269. For the French text, see *Jean Santeuil*, 169. In a letter Proust wrote to Daniel Halévy during this same period to defend himself against the latter's accusations of pederasty, Proust also cites the example of Socrates, along with that of Montaigne, to justify ardent friendships among young men; see *Correspondance*, 1:123, also cited in Diesbach, *Proust*, 74–5.

6. "You can tell anything," Proust famously told the skeptical Gide, "but on condition that you never say: *I.*" *Journals of André Gide*, 2:265.

instinct only, the jellyfish used to revolt me at Balbec; but if I had the eyes to regard them, like Michelet, from the standpoint of natural history and aesthetics, I saw an exquisite blue girandole" (2:650; 3:28).

Proust's insistent analogy between jellyfish (in French, *la méduse*) and homosexuality should perhaps be read as an implicit commentary on the petrifying effect of feminization. In any case, the repetition of this idiosyncratic lesson in natural history, among other arguments too numerous to detail here, from "Avant la nuit" to *Sodome et Gomorrhe I*, makes it clear that Françoise's plight is to be taken as a case in point for tolerance of alternative sexuality rather than a case in itself. Except for the maternal element, lesbianism figures in this story not as a specifically feminine perversion but as a representative of homosexuality in general, or else simply as a transposition of male homosexuality.

A continuum can be traced from "Violante" through "Confession" to "Avant la nuit," linking *manque de volonté* to matricide, and through suicide (which was conventionally seen during this period as a logical response to the shame of deviant sexuality) to homosexuality. "Confession" showcases the themes of matricide and *manque de volonté* which play minor roles in "Violante," while the suicidal narrative that is taken up in "Confession" from "Avant la nuit," which it was written to replace, demonstrates that Proust was experimenting with variations on interrelated themes. These were obsessively to recur, parceled out among different characters, throughout his later work. In the *Recherche,* the mother-tormenting failure of will becomes the protagonist's not quite fatal flaw, while matricide and homosexuality are linked, as we shall see, chiefly through the character of Mlle Vinteuil. *Jean Santeuil,* in the meantime, provides an interim connection between the early depiction of lesbianism in "Avant la nuit" and its function in the *Recherche.*

Jean Santeuil

Jean Santeuil, the unfinished, fragmentary novel that Proust worked on in the late 1890s (and that was not pieced together until the 1950s, by Bernard de Fallois) prefigures the *Recherche* in innumerable ways and, unsurprisingly, reads like a bridge between the early texts of the *Plaisirs et les jours* period and the later work. The proto-novel contains, for instance, the portrait of a Charlus-like figure, the vicomte de Lomperolles, who is devoted to his wife and rails against the effeminacy of contemporary youth; he is later unmasked as an invert when he commits suicide in the wake of a blackmail campaign.[7] Similarly, lesbianism figures in one scene in a manner that at once echoes its function in the earlier texts as a front for male homosexuality and anticipates the Gomorrah of the *Recherche*.

The passage in question reads in part as a rehearsal for the scene in which Swann interrogates Odette about her experiences with other women. Whereas Swann receives an anonymous letter informing him of Odette's less than impeccable behavior, Jean finds out about his girlfriend's lesbian past simply by asking her whether she has "ever . . . you know what I mean . . . before you did with me?" (652; 810). Like the lesbian in "Avant la nuit," she is called Françoise.[8] Under pressure, she eventually admits to having had sex with her friend Charlotte. In subsequent passages Jean falls out of love with Françoise and takes up with Charlotte herself, a switch that prefigures the narrator's interest in Andrée in the *Recherche*.

For the most part, the scene with Françoise sketches, almost verbatim, Swann's interrogation of Odette; even his cri du coeur, "What is really terrible is what one can't imagine," appears in the form of Jean's remark that "the awful thing is not knowing" (653; 811). Indeed, the difference between the two statements encapsulates the way in which this passage shares the tone of the scene from *Un Amour de Swann* without, however, conveying its depth. Jean merely expresses the contingent frustration of not knowing about his

7. See Marcel Proust, *Jean Santeuil*, trans. Gerard Hopkins (New York: Simon & Schuster, 1956), 497–98; 696–97; Pléiade edition, 676–77; 718–19. Subsequent references to these sources will be given consecutively in the text.

8. The name Françoise recurs with obsessive frequency in Proust's writing before being assigned to the housekeeper in the *Recherche*. It is particularly interesting, given the latter's complicated character and important role in the novel, that the women who bear the name in the early works are invariably highly sexualized: the lesbian in "Avant la nuit," the lovesick protagonist in "Mélancolique Villégiature de Mme de Breyves," the love interests in "La Fin de la jalousie" and *Jean Santeuil*. Jean Cocteau remarks that Proust's most original creations are Charlus and Françoise (*Past Tense*, 249).

mistress's past life, while Swann's poignant exclamation implies the impossibility of the male observer's ever penetrating the mystery of female sexuality. The most salient difference between the two scenes is Françoise's concluding soliloquy, which harks back to "Avant la nuit." No trace of this sort of confessional narrative is to be found in any of the scenes in the *Recherche* in which Swann and then the narrator try to elicit the truth about their respective girlfriends' relations with other women. Initially, like Odette, Françoise insists that while she may have done such things, she does not remember when, how often, where, or with whom. Once she has admitted that her previous lover was Charlotte, however, instead of continuing to stonewall à la Odette or Albertine, she suddenly gives voice to a confessional speech about her "flaw" and "the knowledge that I am living a lie." For Charlotte, she says, their amorous interlude was "just a moment's madness," whereas homosexuality is Françoise's "nature" (654; 812). Like her predecessor in "Avant la nuit," Françoise portrays herself as "predisposed" to this sort of love." (These early stories contain the rare moments in Proust's writing where he invokes the distinction, of which much has always been made by sexologists, and which forms the basis of the Kinsey scale continuum, between innate and contingent homosexuality.)

In the face of Jean's continued prurient interest, Françoise describes the history of her guilty secret in terms that recall "Avant la nuit," and even more vividly prefigure "La Race des Tantes": "I have been wretched ever since I first realized that I had that vice," she begins, and goes on to describe the first manifestations of her "vice" in school. When older girls tried to "corrupt" her by describing their assignations with boys, Françoise recounts, she at first misinterpreted the nature of her arousal as being inflamed by her schoolmates' accounts of their heterosexual experiences rather than by the girls themselves: "And when I glutted myself on the smouldering or laughing eyes of my companions, pressed myself against them, embraced them with all my strength, I only thought that I was achieving a sort of communion with willing accomplices, that what was to come would be a shared pleasure. You will never know the full extent of my sufferings" (655; 813).[9]

9. I have modified this translation somewhat in order to highlight its textual similarity to the passages that follow.

Françoise goes on to recount that she had subsequently been beaten up by friends as well as snubbed as a result of her deviance; seeking help, she was ignored by her priest and called insane by her doctor. Nonetheless, she concludes with pride, she has managed to overcome her inclinations and for ten years has hardly been troubled by temptations or stirred by memories of such encounters. Jean's sole reply to this speech, which manifestly tells him at once more and less than he wants to know, is to ask whether her fleeting memories are of Charlotte. Understandably, Françoise is infuriated and refuses to discuss the matter further; the passage concludes on this note.

This scene in *Jean Santeuil,* which resembles nothing so much as a dialogue between an oenophile and a devout adherent of Alcoholics Anonymous, dramatizes the major shift in Proust's depiction of lesbianism. The most discordant note in Françoise's narrative—surely even the most narrow-minded of fin-de-siècle schoolgirls did not routinely beat one another up for such transgressions—betrays the origins of this peroration as a plea for acceptance of male homosexuality. It is also clear from this episode why, at least in terms of sexual dynamics, *Jean Santeuil* never quite gets off the ground, even if much of the text reads like an incomplete jigsaw puzzle version of the *Recherche.* Although the element of the male lover's jealousy of a female rival is present, lesbianism has yet to become truly something other than a transposed simulacrum of male inversion. The inappropriateness of Jean's response to Françoise's impassioned confession reveals the essentially incoherent nature of the passage, which is at bottom two different scenarios soldered together. Jean and Françoise are acting from two unrelated scripts: his belongs to decadent romanticism, hers to social realism. More to the point, he is rehearsing a scene from *Un Amour de Swann* or *La Prisonnière,* while she tries out for *Sodome et Gomorrhe I.*

In fact, the crux of Françoise's speech reappears in various versions of "La Race des Tantes" before finding its final form as part of the essay on inversion in *Sodome et Gomorrhe I* in the unambiguously masculine form of a boy pressing himself against a schoolmate and mistaking his excitation for heterosexual desire: "For no one can tell at first that he is an invert, or a poet, or a snob, or a scoundrel. The boy who has been reading erotic poetry or looking at obscene pictures, if he then presses his body against a schoolfellow's, imagines himself only to be communing with him in an identical desire for a woman" (2:646; 3:25).[10]

The scene between Jean and Françoise is followed by a passage in which, still smitten, he tries to prevent her from seeing Charlotte at the theater, much as the narrator of the *Recherche* expends much effort trying to make sure that Albertine does not see Léa and her friends, or Mlle Vinteuil and hers. He then falls out of love with her and takes up with Charlotte, among others.

Jean drops Françoise as Proust drops the concept of lesbianism as parallel to male inversion. If neither attachment endures, it is doubtless not because Jean is a more fickle character than his fictional successor, but because Françoise, as depicted here, cannot survive as an object of Proustian desire. First, she lacks obscurity, having already delivered her secret, and, what is more, conquered her vagrant desires. Second, and relatedly, she is an invert. She can present no erotic mystery after this scene, and no challenge: she cannot be an *être de fuite,* because, after the manner of inverts, she is in flight only from herself.

Mademoiselle Vinteuil

The trajectory I have been tracing does not stop at the inception of the *Recherche.* The depiction of lesbianism continues to change in the course of the novel, and though we first encounter what eventually becomes Gomorrah in "Combray," the shape that it finally assumes does not become clear—to the extent that clarity ever characterizes Proust's portrayal of female sexuality—until much later. In the beginning there is Mlle Vinteuil.

Mlle Vinteuil seems at first glance to correspond to the inversion model, which is doubtless one of the reasons why critics have assumed

10. See Esquisse I, the earliest version of "La Race des Tantes," where two distinct variations on precisely the same idea can be found, one in a passage on the erotic history of Hubert de Guerchy, prototype of Charlus (3:929), the other in generalized, hypothetical form as in the final version (3:930–31). The Guerchy version closely resembles Françoise's speech, except that it is in the third person.

that Proust's lesbians are really boys in disguise, and that his Gomorrah corresponds to his Sodom. From her initial appearance she is described as being in some essential and evident sense a boy. She is not, however, an *invertie*. Instead, she is a tomboy, one whose rough exterior seems to hide a more feminine nature. In fact, Mlle Vinteuil is depicted in terms that suggest the male inversion model, the "anima muliebris in corpore virili inclusa," rather than its complement. The narrator's grandmother—who, as we shall see in the next chapter, has a keen eye for hidden femininity—quickly discerns the shy girl beneath Mlle Vinteuil's apparent virility: "My grandmother had drawn our attention to the gentle, delicate, almost timid expression which might often be caught flitting across the freckled face of this otherwise stolid child" (1:122–23; 1:112).

The description of Mlle Vinteuil is imbued with an androgyny that is emphasized each time her name appears. A subtle sexual asymmetry, and an exception to the normative depiction of deviance that has been found in the *Recherche,* are thus written into it from the first. When we are told that Charlus's peculiarity can be explained by his being at heart a woman, we have already encountered such a creature, and in the form of an actual woman. Mlle Vinteuil, too, despite all her apparent masculinity, is "really" a girl. This paradox follows the structure of the narrator's misapprehension concerning the color of Gilberte's eyes: just as the narrator might not have been "so especially enamored" of the latter's blue eyes had they not actually been so very black, it is only because Mlle Vinteuil is so very much a boy that her girlishness causes comment (on Gilberte's eyes, see 1:153; 1:139). One of the main differences between her warring genders and those of Charlus is that hers appear simultaneously rather than successively: "One would see in clear outline, as though in a transparency, beneath the mannish face of the 'good sort' [*bon diable*] that she was, the finer features of a young woman in tears" (1:123; 1:112). The description of Mlle Vinteuil does not evolve aesthetically to reveal hidden facets, since her hidden facets are on display from the beginning. On the contrary, as we shall see, the only development her character undergoes is a process of desexualization.

Although the description of Mlle Vinteuil should fit somewhere into the system of inversion that is invoked several volumes after her initial appearance, she does not embody any model of female sexual inversion.

Rather, as Brigitte Mahuzier points out, she represents moral inversion: instead of being a man trapped in the body of a woman, Mlle Vinteuil is a masochist trapped in the body of a sadist.[11] Her masculine and feminine components do not exclude each other, as in the portrayal of Charlus, whose hyperbolic masculinity is revealed to be a front for his essential femininity, the latter becoming increasingly apparent as he ages. Neither aspect of Mlle Vinteuil, it seems, is exactly a sham; her boyish and girlish traits coexist as if they were a pair of fraternal twins sharing a single body. If Mlle Vinteuil recalls Proust's earlier writings, it is not so much because of her masculinity—again, she is no *invertie*—as that she represents parental profanation. What happens at Montjouvain is in many ways a recreation of "La Confession d'une jeune fille." It is entirely clear that Mlle Vinteuil's sexuality is what kills her father, and it is also clear that M. Vinteuil is a highly maternal figure. Long widowed, he has fully assumed a maternal stance in his devotion to his daughter. The narrator's mother, who, like the mothers in "Violante" and "Confession," suffers as a result of her child's *manque de volonté,* explicitly identifies with M. Vinteuil in his role as *mater dolorosa:* "My mother had not forgotten the sad last years of M. Vinteuil's life, his complete absorption, first in having to play mother and nursery-maid to his daughter, and, later, in the suffering she had caused him" (1:174; 1:157).

M. Vinteuil does not even escape implication in his daughter's debauchery: parental profanation occurs on a textual level as well as in the form of desecration of the father's photograph. Before M. Vinteuil's death, rumors circulate in Combray (and, therefore, in "Combray") about the sort of "music" made at Montjouvain by Mlle Vinteuil, the ill-reputed "friend" who moves in with them, and the father as well. "They play too much music, those people, in my opinion," says one local wag, to the general hilarity of all, including the local priest; "I met Papa Vinteuil the other day, by the cemetery. It was all he could do to keep on his feet" (1:161; 1:146).

Even though we know that the old music teacher has gone piously to the cemetery to pay homage to his late wife, and that he is not far from joining her, M. Vinteuil himself, through the narrator's reproduction of

11. Brigitte Mahuzier, "Proust and the Ethics of Sadomasochism," forthcoming.

village gossip, becomes part of the unsavory goings-on that bring about his death. Whether or not anyone actually believes that the Montjouvain *ménage* is really *à trois* in any but the most literal sense, the old man's image is sullied by his daughter's perversion long before his photograph is incorporated into her sinister foreplay ritual with her corrupt "friend."

The Nameless Friend

Mlle Vinteuil's friend, although she has no name and is never described—initially her only stated quality is her bad reputation—plays a key role in the *Recherche*. If any character embodies the interdependence of high and low, the link between the baseness of deviant sexuality and the transcendence of art, it is she. When the narrator says in introducing the Montjouvain scene that what follows would play an important role in his life for reasons that will become clear much later, he is not just referring to Albertine's revelation of her connection with the two women. The scene's ramifications go further still: to the very heart of the novel's most privileged theme of redemption in art. It is because of Mlle Vinteuil's friend, nameless like the narrator himself, that Vinteuil's greatness becomes known to posterity.[12] It is also only because of the painstaking transcription of his work to which she devotes the rest of her life that the narrator is able to hear the septet that becomes an important model of artistic production in the *Recherche,* the final panel of the multimedia triptych featuring Elstir's paintings and Bergotte's novels.

When he first hears the septet, the narrator reflects on the ironies of how it had been saved through the ministrations of the same person who had caused its composer's demise, and also of her mixed role in his own

12. Monique Wittig has pointed out the link between Mlle Vinteuil's friend and the narrator which is implied by their common namelessness (keynote speech at Duke University conference on gender and sexuality in Romance studies, February 1995). Early versions of the Montjouvain story suggest that Proust originally intended to name her: she is successively called Mlle X, Mlle Y, and Mlle Anna in Esquisse LII (see 1:803–4), but in the final draft she is never referred to as anything other than "Mlle Vinteuil's friend."

life. Through MlleVinteuil's friend he connects his morbid obsession with Albertine's sexuality to the hope the music inspires in him of an eventual salvation in art. For him as for M.Vinteuil, he muses, she has caused great suffering, and yet for him too her role is inextricably double:

> It was thanks to her, in compensation, that I had been able to apprehend the strange summons which I should henceforth never cease to hear, as the promise and proof that there existed something other, realisable no doubt through art, than the nullity that I had found in all my pleasures and in love itself, and that if my life seemed to me so futile, at least it had not yet accomplished everything. (3:264-65; 3:767)

He thus explicitly links Gomorrah, through MlleVinteuil's friend, to what is meant to transcend all that it most sordidly represents. This irony was already in place from the first drafts of the Montjouvain scene. It is a salient example of the form of paradox of which Proust was most fond, the "Gilberte's eyes" paradigm according to which things seem to be themselves only insofar as they are actually (or also) their opposite: Legrandin would not rail against snobbery were he not himself secretly a snob; Charlus displays exaggeratedly rigorous masculinity because he is "really" a woman; and so on. It is this love of the amplified paradox in Proust that led Aldous Huxley to label him "La Rochefoucauld magnified ten thousand times."[13] To this extent Gomorrah, at least as exemplified by the "demoiselles Vinteuil," as Charlus calls them (3:223; 3:728), represents what is most predictably Proustian about Proust—the *Recherche* of the first and last volumes—and it is in part for this reason that critics have not seen beyond Mlle Vinteuil and her friend in accounting for Proust's depiction of lesbianism.[14]

Mlle Vinteuil and her friend, however, do not really exemplify Gomorrah; they are merely related to it. In the end, they represent lesbianism in its most domesticated, acceptable form. If, as I have been arguing, the

13. See Aldous Huxley, "Books for the Journey," in *Selected Essays* (London: Chatto & Windus, 1961), 38.

14. When Walter Benjamin refers to "the lesbian scene from Proust" in his *Moscow Diary,* for instance, he clearly means the Montjouvain scene. See Walter Benjamin, *Moscow Diary,* trans. Richard Sieburth (Cambridge: Harvard University Press, 1986), 94–95.

Montjouvain scene, with its emphasis on parental profanation, harks back to a period in Proust's career in which female sexuality doubled for male homosexuality, the last glimpse we get of the Vinteuil couple reproduces the comfortable sexlessness (or at least perceived sexlessness) of the nineteenth-century "Boston marriage." In *La Prisonnière* the two women are described as having overcome their unhealthy desires in order finally to achieve a friendship unclouded by eroticism: "Those morbidly carnal relations, that troubled, smouldering conflagration, had gradually given way to the flame of a pure and lofty friendship" (3:263; 3:765–66).

In an early version of what would become the Montjouvain scene, this sexless resolution to the young women's unhinged sexuality is developed in greater detail: "A few years ago, I met at Mme Verdurin's Mlle Vington, who had become an old maid, with her friend. Of their forgotten games had been born an affection such as there should be, such as there rarely is, between sisters, with all the heroism and saintliness that abnegation, disinterest, delicate tenderness, respect, and deathless devotion can bring about."[15] Mlle Vinteuil (*née* Vington)[16] and her friend thus represent, at least in early drafts, perhaps the most successful couple in the novel. Charlus and Jupien also remain together, but the latter's role becomes that of a nanny, as the baron grows increasingly blind and senile and has to be rescued from more and more embarrassingly inappropriate pickup attempts.[17] But the demoiselles Vintueil endure as a couple only at the price of a desexualization that resembles the fate of some lesbian couples in *The Pure and the Impure:* their relations eventually shade into sisterly intimacy.[18] Sisterly intimacy itself, it should be noted, is called into question in a peculiar throwaway remark early in *Sodome et Gomorrhe II* which

---

15. "Or il y a quelques années, je rencontrai chez Mme Verdurin Mlle Vington devenue vieille fille, avec son amie. Des jeux oubliés d'autrefois était née entre elles une affection comme devait être, comme est rarement celle de deux soeurs, avec tout ce que l'abnégation, le désintéressement, la tendresse délicate, le respect, le dévouement au-delà de la mort peut faire fleurir de plus héroïque, de plus saint." Esquisse LI, 1:801.

16. In even earlier drafts the family name is Lignon.

17. For a more detailed discussion, see Chapter 2, n.32.

18. "In living amorously together, two women may eventually discover that their mutual attraction is not basically sensual." Colette, *Pure and the Impure,* 111.

bizarrely suggests that incestuous lesbian relations were taken in stride in high society, and even accomodated by hosts planning sleeping arrangements for overnight visits: "There is no vice that does not find ready tolerance in the best society, and one has seen a country house turned upside down in order that two sisters might sleep in adjoining rooms as soon as their hostess learned that theirs was a more than sisterly affection" (2:742; 3:114).

Sisterhood, as depicted by Proust, was unexpectedly powerful among the aristocracy of the time.[19] In any case, the asexual purity that the relation between Mlle Vinteuil and her friend takes on has, especially in the early drafts, a hyperbolic air about it which implies that they have crossed the binary divide and entered the realm of (generally maternal) figures who are entirely and selflessly devoted to their loved ones. Indeed, the friend, in one of the preliminary versions, has been, in a sense, widowed and has taken up M. Vinteuil's habit of daily visits to the cemetery:

Mlle Vington died last year. Her friend did not expect to have to survive her. She lives exclusively at [Montjouvain] and, I am told, goes every day to the Combray cemetery, to weep before a small plot containing three tombs. The first is that of M. Vington. The second, his daughter's, has these words on it: "I await you." The third is the one in which she promised Mlle Vington on her deathbed she would be buried. It seems she won't make her wait long now.[20]

Proust's decision not to include this passage in the final version of his novel may have been due to its uncharacteristically mawkish tone (as well

---

19. Proust went through two other configurations before arriving at his lesbian incest example: first he posited the couple as a brother and a sister, then as two brothers (see variants, 3:1389).

20. "Mlle Vington est morte l'année dernière. Son amie ne pensait pas devoir la survivre. Elle vit tout à fait à [Montjouvain] et va, m'a-t-on dit, tous les jours au cimetière de Combray, pleurer devant un petit enclos qui contient trois tombes. La première est celle de M. Vington. La seconde, celle de sa fille, porte ces mots: 'Je t'attends'. La troisième est celle où elle a promis à Mlle Vington à son lit de mort de se faire enterrer. Il semble qu'elle ne doive plus longtemps la faire attendre." Esquisse LI, 1:801.

as the unwittingly gruesome note of the epitaph), but it is also possible that he chose to suppress such a sentimental and celebratory conclusion to the story of Montjouvain. Also missing from the final form of the coda to the Vinteuil family saga is the note in this same draft on the utter selflessness of the friend in completing the father's work: Mlle Vinteuil (here Vington) having lost her fortune, her friend publishes it at her own expense, and insists on anonymity (1:801).

Thus the namelessness that is the textual fate of Mlle Vinteuil's friend in the *Recherche* finds its justification in her refusal to name herself. In her extreme modesty, which is evidently meant to serve as a counterpoint to her earlier savage eroticism, she resembles the man whose death she effectively caused; and it also links her to the first model of purity and self-effacement in the novel, the grandmother.

The story of Montjouvain therefore contains the full paradox that Proust originally set out to invest in sexual relations between women: both the extreme depravity of parental profanation and the other face of that coin, the selfless devotion that makes Mlle Vinteuil's friend resemble, ultimately, the man whose photograph she has spat on, and leads her to spend years of her life deciphering his works. As the narrator notes in *La Prisonnière*, "Her adoration of her father was the very condition of his daughter's sacrilege," and Mlle Vinteuil's friend has absorbed the cult of the father as the necessary condition of her pleasure in profaning his image (3:263; 3:765). As he further remarks in the same passage, this profound and apparently paradoxical tie between genius, talent, and even virtue on the one hand and "the sheath of vices" in which they are contained on the other is hardly unique to the Vinteuil clan (3:265–66; 3:768).

The fact that the narrator is able to hear the Vinteuil septet played at the Verdurins' is due just as much, he points out, to Charlus's patronage of Morel's musical skills as to the years the friend has spent transcribing the composer's music. In calling attention to the ultimate banality of this seemingly unusual situation in which a father's debasement by his daughter leads to his artistic redemption at the hands of her illicit lover, Proust, or at least his narrator, assimilates lesbianism into the great paradox mill of the *Recherche*. In this way, too, the Montjouvain scene takes up where the writings of the 1890s leave off: lesbianism is, if not "simply" a displacement of male homosexuality, at least one more instance of things being at once precisely what they seem and their contrary.

Montjouvain therefore both assures lesbianism its central place in the novel and relegates it to the margins, as yet another lesson, albeit an important one, in how virtue is wedded to vice and greatness to depravity. Nonetheless, even if this is the function Proust had marked out for Gomorrah before it was ever called Gomorrah, once named as such it began to take on a life of its own. In Chapter 5 I will show how female homoeroticism in the *Recherche* is based on a relation to the mother that diverges from the monolithic matricidal guilt of Proust's early works. Here, I analyze the unique specificity of Gomorrhean sexuality as it departs from the familiar themes that we have seen emerging from the earlier writings, including the Montjouvain drama.

Morel: A Crisis of Definition

One of the most disconcerting moments in the novel occurs when Charlus opens a letter addressed to Morel, only to discover that his male lover is, somehow, a lesbian. The letter, sent by the actress Léa, "notorious for her exclusive taste for women," is written in an unmistakably passionate tone and refers to its addressee in the feminine (3:212; 3:720). Charlus is most disturbed by Léa's use of the expression *en être:* "Of course you are one of us, you pretty sweetheart [ma belle chérie, toi tu en es au moins]," she writes. What perplexes Charlus is the question of exactly whom "us" refers to in all this: he had thought he knew what *en être* meant, whereas Léa's letter suggests not merely that his boyfriend has been unfaithful to him, but that he has been so in a manner that the baron cannot even imagine, and that shakes him to the core of his own self-definition: "What most disturbed the Baron was the phrase 'one of us.' Ignorant at first of its application, he had eventually, now many moons ago, learned that he himself was 'one of them.' And now this notion that he had acquired was thrown back into question" (3:212; 3:720).

Charlus is now faced with jealousy of women—something of which he had never conceived—as well as of men. The extent to which this revelation disturbs both Charlus and the sexual equilibrium of the novel becomes clear when the narrator, soon after this passage, denies what he has already identified as its import: "It was of men alone that M. de Charlus was capable of feeling any jealousy as far as Morel was concerned. Women inspired in him none whatsoever" (3:214; 3:722).

Charlus's revelation that Gomorrah poses a threat to Sodom calls into question the system of sexual definition relied upon not just by the baron but by the novel itself. This much is indicated by the narrator's flagrant self-contradiction. Women in general are not the problem; it is Gomorrah that upsets the delicate sexual balance in place since *Sodome et Gomorrhe I.* Morel has not been portrayed as exclusively homosexual, and Charlus is proud, not jealous, of his lover's reputation as a ladykiller. Léa's letter, though, suggests something else: that Morel is not so much bisexual as tri-sexual. It is not his excursions into heterosexuality that bother Charlus. On the contrary, because his lover seduces women, Charlus can believe that he himself has escaped inversion into homosexuality, since his boyfriend is a "real man," a ladies' man. According to his flawed theory, which mistakes inversion for homosexuality, his lover's manliness must mean that he, too, is manly, whereas the narrator knows that Morel's manliness points instead to Charlus's girlishness. But what the baron finds threatening is Morel's alleged and incomprehensible lesbianism: "The baron, in the face of this novel meaning of a phrase that was so familiar to him, felt himself tormented by an anxiety of the mind as well as of the heart, born of this twofold mystery which combined an extension of the field of his jealousy with the sudden inadequacy of a definition" (3:212; 3:721).

Léa's letter to Morel causes in Charlus the same sort of vertiginous stupefaction that Swann and the narrator experience on learning of their respective girlfriends' lesbian inclinations. In each case what is particularly troubling to the jealous lover is an almost algebraic disturbance in the distribution of sameness and difference: the rival does not resemble the lover; no neat substitution may be imagined. Still, the concept that a woman may have sex with other women is not unknown. Although Albertine's enigmatic desires suffuse the later volumes of the novel with an epistemological anxiety that is quelled only when the narrator gives up his quest to understand her in favor of more lofty pursuits, the possibility that she prefers women cannot in itself present the sort of intellectual challenge that Charlus faces when he hears of Morel's membership in the secret society of Gomorrah. After all, male lesbianism is no more a category outside the book than within its pages—even less so, in fact.[21]

In *Sodome et Gomorrhe I,* Proust seems to set the stage for Charlus's discovery about Morel when he (or his narrator) discusses various forms of male inversion. Some men, he notes, do not care what sort of pleasure they receive so long as they take it with a man, "whereas others, whose sensuality is doubtless more violent, feel an imperious need to localise their physical pleasure" (2:645; 3:23–24). It is once again testimony to Proust's remarkable lack of phallocentricity—as well as something of an anatomical riddle—that these male inverts whose desires are so physically specific should also be those whose inclinations run to both men and women.[22] They do not seek out just any women, though: "the second sort seek out those women who love other women, who can procure for them a young man, enhance the pleasure they experience in his company; better still, they can, in the same fashion, enjoy with such women the same pleasure as with a man" (2:645; 3:24).

Especially since the passage then goes on to discuss the nuances of jealousy for female rivals that this sort of homosexual inspires in his male lovers, the description would seem to anticipate the revelation of Morel's peculiar sexuality. It does so, however, only up to a point. This portrayal of the second variety of invert is a kind of mirror image of Morel, with the emphasis in his case being on the feminine rather than the masculine side of things. The "second sort" of invert enjoys sexual relations with lesbians notably because he treats them as if they were men. Morel, in contrast, according to Léa's letter, acts like a woman with her; she is able to have sex with Morel despite her exclusive taste for women because Morel, for her, *is* somehow a woman. The passage on inversion from *Sodome et Gomorrhe I* describes the jealousy that such relations provoke: "The jealous friend suffers from the feeling that the man he loves is riveted to the woman who is to him almost a man, and at the same time feels his beloved almost escape him because, to these women, he is something which the lover himself cannot conceive, a sort of woman" (2:646; 3:24).

21. Gide does come up with the rubric "male lesbian," but it does not correspond to Morel's case (see Chapter 2, n.26).

22. See Silverman's discussion of the implications of this passage in *Male Subjectivity,* 381–82.

As the repetition of "almost" in this passage and its confusing interplay of pronouns underscore, the configuration described here is not a simple one. Nor does it fully correspond to Morel's situation. Not only does he, to all appearances, participate enthusiastically in Léa's and her friends' conception of him as one of them, but also he turns the other stated interest of such men in such women on its head. Instead of using lesbians as a lure for procuring young men, as the passage from *Sodome et Gomorrhe I* describes, Morel allows himself, according to Andrée, to be used by Albertine for seducing young women "who would fall for a boy but might not have responded to a girl's advances" (3:612–13; 4:179).

One possible explanation for the discrepancy between the second type of invert in *Sodome et Gomorrhe I* and the character to whom the description would most clearly seem to apply lies in the taxonomic passage itself. The two categories of male homosexual—those who seek unspecified pleasures only with men and those who desire to engage in specific acts but are willing to carry them out with women who like other women as well as with men—are not the only specimens the passage has to offer. The narrator goes on to allude to other types of male inversion, noting that each will be dealt with in turn: "Let us, finally, leave until later the men who have sealed a pact with Gomorrah," he says, promising that such men will be discussed when Charlus encounters them (2:646; 3:25). Since this promise occurs on the page following the description of the second type of invert, we can only surmise that those men who have made a pact with Gomorrah are not the same as those men who seek lesbians because they can treat them like men and use them as bait for picking up boys. Morel does not quite belong to this category, the difference being that instead of using women as men and for men, he seems, at least temporarily, to have gone over to the other side.

As we saw in Chapter 1, in the essay "À propos de Baudelaire," Proust likens Morel to Baudelaire in his role as "liaison between Sodom and Gomorrah." The lines he cites from "Lesbos" show the poetic persona as a sort of resident alien on Lesbian soil. For Morel to have concluded a pact with Gomorrah entails dual citizenship—or, again, not bisexuality so much as trisexuality. It is not a coincidence that the term "Gomorrah" does not appear in the passage on inverts who like women who prefer women. Two types of lesbianism seem to coexist in Proust's writing. The first type is more anodyne, to the extent that it is predictable even in its vicious, profanatory mode. As the example of Mlle Vinteuil demonstrates, this kind of perversion operates on the binary model of Proustian paradox, which is also the logic of inversion. Its "sadism" depends on an essential goodness, just as Charlus's hypermasculinity depends on his essential femininity. As the narrator observes after the Montjouvain scene, "Sadists of Mlle Vinteuil's sort are creatures so purely sentimental, so naturally virtuous, that even sensual pleasure appears to them as something bad, the prerogative of the wicked" (1:179; 1:162).

The second type goes by the name Gomorrah. It is not subject to the laws of Proustian paradox. Albertine can never be shown to contain her own opposite, because she does not allow herself to be defined in the first place; Andrée never ceases changing her story, so that she is perhaps the novel's most successful liar; Léa, famous for her exclusive taste for women, does not betray her preference even when she includes a man among her girlfriends. This form of female homosexuality is so potent, so excessive and uncontainable, as to infect not only the realm of putatively heterosexual women (Odette, Mme Verdurin) but Sodom as well.

Albertine's Orifices

The enduring enigma posed by Albertine's sexuality is perhaps nowhere so opaque as in the passage late in *La Prisonnière* in which she expresses, or at least seems to begin to express, in the most vulgar terms the narrator can imagine, a desire to be sodomized. This moment is, of course, much less unfathomable if one subscribes to the reading of Albertine as a transposition of some actual or hypothetical Albert. And yet even so the episode presents difficulties.

What happens is this: returning from the Verdurin salon where he has heard the Vinteuil septet, and where he prevented Albertine from going for fear she would encounter the Vinteuil girls, the narrator quarrels with her over her relations with various women. Finally, irritated by his condescending offer of money so that she can play at being *la dame chic* and invite the Verdurins to dinner, Albertine says: "Thank you for nothing! Spend money on them! I'd a great deal rather you left me free for once in a way to go and get myself . . . [*me faire casser . . .*]." At this point she stops suddenly, blushes, and puts her hands to her mouth as if to take back her words (3:343; 3:840). She then offers various implausible explanations of what she had meant, but is unable to divert the narrator from his insistence on deciphering her phrase. For three pages he attempts to reconstruct her meaning in an interpretive labor as painstaking as that of Mlle Vinteuil's friend to establish the correct text of the late composer's work.

Finally the missing piece falls into place: "le pot." What Albertine had apparently wanted to do was "aller se faire casser le pot," an extremely vulgar term for passive anal intercourse. Like Charlus faced with Léa's anomalous use of *en être,* the narrator is disturbed as much by the expression itself as by what it designates:

> Horror! It was this that she would have preferred. Twofold horror! For even the vilest of prostitutes, who consents to such a thing, or even desires it, does not use that hideous expression to the man who indulges in it. She would feel it too degrading. To a woman alone, if she loves women, she might say it, to excuse herself for giving herself presently to a man. (3:345–46; 3:843)

The narrator thus somewhat bizarrely takes Albertine's expression of desire to be sodomized as further proof of her lesbianism. How are we to read this scene?[23]

Even if the act in question is more readily associated with male homosexuality than with lesbianism, Albertine's remark does not make a great deal more sense in the mouth of an Albert, since sodomy is what sodomites presumably indulge in already. In any case, whether we read the scene as homosexual or heterosexual, what Albertine seeks is still something that she could in principle get right there at home.[24] Ultimately, this

---

23. Jean Cocteau, who claims to have met the "stupid bellboy" on whom the *prisonnière* is based, laments Proust's "naïveté" in having written this scene without realizing that "a woman, and even less a *jeune fille* (and one who likes women), cannot utter such a phrase. On the other hand, it is exactly in the style of his bellboy." Cocteau, *Past Tense,* 258 (translation modified slightly).

24. See Sedgwick's discussion of this scene in *Epistemology of the Closet,* 238–40.

moment illustrates the sheer outrageousness, the excessiveness of a sexuality whose demand, at least when directed at a male partner, can never be met by supply. In this sense Gomorrah represents a variant of the familiar Baudelairean theme of female sexual insatiability. The Baudelairean intertext that best accounts for Gomorrah is therefore "Sed non satiata," in which the poetic persona's inability to match his mistress's boundless desires is linked to her lesbian inclinations, rather than "Lesbos" or "Delphine et Hippolyte."[25]

Albertine's expression of desire to "se faire casser le pot" is roughly equivalent, in its incomprehensible otherness, to Morel's letter from Léa as read by Charlus. In both cases what is revealed to the horrified onlooker is an erotic discourse that shocks not by what it designates physically so much as by what the tone of the words suggests. The narrator is no more the implied addressee of Albertine's announcement than Charlus is of Léa's letter: it is clear that Albertine has "forgotten herself" and is speaking as if to someone else. As in the letter, both speaker and implied addressee are evidently meant, somehow, to be female, and in both cases it is this aspect that renders the discourse incomprehensible. It does not matter that what Albertine says she wants is not in fact something that anatomically excludes the narrator. As in the letter that Charlus opens, the physical laws of sex are not in question. At stake is a sexuality that is by definition exclusively female, and by that same token inaccessible and incomprehensible to the male lover who happens to catch a glimpse into its murky and otherwise unsuspected depths.

It is perhaps not enough to say that the physical laws of sex are not at issue here. This passage may be shocking to the reader (for the reader's surprise must necessarily diverge in this instance from the narrator's) because it strains verisimilitude, or because of its unexpected raunchiness; indeed, this is one of the very few sexually specific moments in the book.[26] But what makes it memorably problematic is that it so flagrantly flouts the laws

---

25. Baudelaire, *Oeuvres complètes*, 1:28. See also Claude Pichois's commentary in this edition (esp. 887).

26. The other vulgar anatomical reference is Jupien's coquettish "What a big bum you have!" addressed to Charlus during their initial seduction scene (2:632; 3:12). Along with various other mentions of characters' backsides, such as the "tense muscular wave" that

of sexual predictability. The word for what Albertine wants is "sodomy"; her announcement defies not only received wisdom about what women do together but also the ostensibly—and ostentatiously—binary foundation of a work whose sexual cornerstone is *Sodome et Gomorrhe*.

As both Sedgwick and Silverman point out, Albertine is elsewhere depicted in terms that suggest that her chief erotic mode is, as the narrator's too seems to be, oral.[27] The passage in which Albertine most evidently displays her orality occurs early in *La Prisonnière* and has been amply discussed by critics. This scene, in which Albertine goes on at bombastic and provocative length about the architectural splendors of the ice cream served at the Ritz, has been the focus of much critical attention because it is both erotically and discursively charged. Her lyrically overblown flight of fancy is the longest speech Albertine makes in the novel. It is also self-consciously "literary," and causes the narrator to reflect that even if he himself would never have spoken in those terms, they nonetheless showcase the extent to which she has been influenced by him. The language she uses, he concludes, testifies to her being his "creation" (3:125; 3:636).

Critics have seen fellatio imagery in Albertine's encomium to ice cream, as she rhapsodizes about columns, pillars, and obelisks of freshness melting in her throat.[28] Philippe Lejeune goes so far as to claim that lesbianism is subsumed by male homosexuality in her speech, its fundamental orality overwhelmed by the insistence on phallic shapes.[29]

The ice cream passage bears comparison to the "casser le pot" episode on a number of points. In both scenes Albertine's desires are on display, and in both cases their discursive expression is what arrests the narrator's attention. In the ice cream passage he is happy to note not the oral eroti-

---

"ripple[s] over Legrandin's rump" (1:135; 1:123) and Charlus's "almost symbolic behind" (2:890; 3:254), these allusions form something of a posterior leitmotif in the novel.

27. See Sedgwick, *Epistemology of the Closet,* 235–37; Silverman, *Male Subjectivity,* 378–88.

28. See Margaret Gray's interesting analysis of critical readings of this passage in *Postmodern Proust,* 104–12.

29. Philippe Lejeune, "Écriture et sexualité," *Europe* (February–March 1971), 135; see also Gray, *Postmodern Proust,* 108. Gray herself reads this passage in terms of Albertine's essential indeterminacy.

cism he shares with her but rather the "literary" language that he identifies as the mark of his own influence. In the "casser le pot" scene his attention is also caught by her language, but here his complacency is shattered because the terms in which she frames her desire betray precisely the opposite of what her earlier speech announced. Here her language is just as clearly acquired, but not from him; rather, her use of the vulgar expression points to her having escaped his influence. She can have learned such language, if not such habits, only in a lesbian underworld, a world in which such acts may or may not be common practice, but in which, in any case, they are referred to in such terms. It is the linguistic otherness of her eroticism that appalls him. What comes across loud and clear in her unfinished announcement is that her sexual grammar has been learned elsewhere.

The ice cream speech and the "casser le pot" scene are the moments in the novel in which Albertine most clearly expresses her own sexuality. If much more critical ink has been spilled over the first than the second, it is surely at least in part because of the extent to which the ice cream speech foregrounds what is thought of as the necessary, predictable condition of lesbian eroticism—orality—while at the same time displaying what can easily be read as a phallic geometry. Albertine's hymn to melting columns of freshness is readily assimilated into an aesthetics of male homosexuality. masquerading as lesbianism. It also, of course, offers a comfortable vision of Albertine as docile pupil, repeating back in parodic form the lessons she has learned from the master. The "casser le pot" scene is much more difficult to characterize, presenting as it does an entirely undomesticated version of female sexuality. Albertine's desire to be what we are accustomed to calling "sodomized" entails not a Sodomization of Gomorrah but, as in Léa's letter, the contrary, for which there exists no name.

Gomorrah thus becomes a sexual anomaly, the site of sexual unpredictability in the *Recherche* and the exception to its stated rules. Léa's letter to Morel, which makes it clear that Sodomites are not safe from Gomorrah, and Albertine's renegade expression of anal eroticism represent the outer limits of this aberrant sexuality. What begins as a clear transposition of male homosexuality in the early works and continues in the Montjouvain scene as a safely domesticated paradox ends up infiltrating Sodom itself, and ultimately demonstrates the insufficiency of received sexual definition.

5

Mothers and Daughters:
The Origins of Gomorrah

$\overset{\backprime}{A}$ la recherche du temps perdu has long provided something of a field day for psychoanalytic criticism. This is partly due to the narrator's own relentless psychologizing, but it stems as well from the fact that much of "Combray" in particular sounds as though it might have been written by Freud himself, under a Gallic pseudonym, to dramatize his theory of the Oedipus complex. It has, accordingly, often been read "as an epic of the Oedipal struggle," as Michael Riffaterre puts it.[1] Seldom has any fictional character been quite so mother-obsessed as Proust's narrator, although it should also be said that the work of no other author besides P. G. Wodehouse features quite so many uncles and aunts and so few parents. Still, a cursory glance at the first books of the Recherche, especially one that takes in the author's biography as well, furnishes much grist for the oedipal mill.

To begin with, Proust famously eradicates in his semiautobiographical novel his actual younger brother, much as Freud's hypothetical little turn-of-the-century Oedipus is most often depicted sibling-free. The father also fades from the narrative, all but eclipsed not long after his initial appearance as an illusive fantasy of the Old Testament patriarch Abraham in

---

1. Michael Riffaterre, "The Intertextual Unconscious," in *The Trials of Psychoanalysis,* ed. Françoise Meltzer (Chicago: University of Chicago Press, 1992), 212.

"Combray." Here, though, is where Proust's text begins to depart from the typical Freudian scenario. Instead of the interdicting role the narrator and tradition expect of him, the father plays that of oedipal enabler, as it were, inviting his wife to share her son's bed and thus paving the way for the debilitating "failure of will" (*manque de volonté*) that will haunt the protagonist throughout the following volumes.

The mother, too, is eventually occulted, replaced by her own mother. The grandmother's taking over of the maternal role in the novel is another element that can be and has been read in Freudian terms: it "defuse[s] the Oedipal conflict and for a time free[s] the narrator from the bondage of rivalry with his father," to use Riffaterre's summary of much of the Proust criticism on the subject.[2] The grandmother who takes over her daughter's role in the novel has consistently been read in biographical terms as a version of Proust's own mother. There is ample extratextual foundation for this reading. The grandmother's death, for instance, as described in *Le Côté de Guermantes II,* bears obvious resemblances to the death of Mme Proust, just as the narrator's reaction to it echoes the author's own devastation at the loss of his mother.

This division of the maternal figure into mother and grandmother has no precedent in Proust's earlier work. The stories of the *Plaisirs et les jours* period contain no grandmaternal characters, nor does *Jean Santeuil,* which, like them, was written while Mme Proust was still living (Proust's maternal grandmother, Mme Nathé Weil, had died in 1890). In the protonovel the stern yet loving presence of the grandmother is taken over by the maternal grandfather, M. Sandré, whose (presumably) late wife is never mentioned. In this sense Proust's early fiction is more unambiguously matricentric than the *Recherche,* which, after "Combray," displaces the maternal center with its division of labor between mother and grandmother.

Biographically it seems clear (if perhaps not, in the end, especially illuminating) that both characters are largely avatars of Mme Proust. Some commentators, though, have suggested that the grandmother in the novel is modeled partly on Proust's maternal grandmother, and it is relevant in the context of the argument I will develop here that the element most

2. Ibid., 216.

often cited in support of this hypothesis is Mme Weil's love of Mme de Sévigné's letters.[3] The problem I address in this chapter does not, however, hinge on biography. It is, rather, the question, what does it mean for Proust to have split the maternal figure in two in the novel?

The interpretation of the grandmother as simply another version of the mother recalls the reading of Gomorrah as a second Sodom, another version of homosexuality created so that the author might examine male inversion from a safe remove. In both the reading of the grandmother as a displaced transposition of the mother (or of Proust's mother) and that of Gomorrah as a displaced transposition of male homosexuality, there is a certain amount of truth, but in both cases the process is much more complicated than is at first apparent. The division of the maternal role between the two characters cannot fully be accounted for as a de-oedipalization of the mother figure; nor does the otherwise compelling argument that Proust could not bring himself directly to describe his mother's death explain entirely the role of the grandmother in the *Recherche*. What escapes these explanations of the grandmother as a sort of defused mother is the novel's emphasis on the very close relationship between the two women. It is, as I will argue, in the relation between grandmother and mother, articulated through citations of the letters written by Mme de Sévigné to her daughter, that the origins of Proust's depiction of Gomorrah can be found.

Madame de Sévigné

From her first appearances in the novel to the moment of her death, the narrator's grandmother quotes Mme de Sévigné. She reads and cites Sé-

3. A letter written by Mme Proust to her son after her mother's death reinforces this conjecture: see Marcel Proust, *Selected Letters*, vol. 1, *1880–1903*, ed. Philip Kolb, trans. Ralph Manheim (New York: Doubleday, 1983), 28. George Painter believes unequivocally that Mme Weil lent to the narrator's grandmother her love of Sévigné, but Painter's insistence on finding direct biographical equivalences for each aspect of the *Recherche* leads him constantly to beg the question of extratextual origin. See George Painter, *Marcel Proust*, 2 vols. (New York: Random House, 1978), 1:76. See also Céleste Albaret, *Monsieur Proust*, trans. Barbara Bray (New York: McGraw-Hill, 1976), 136.

vigné's letters as the very devout read and cite the Bible. She is never without a volume of the seventeenth-century writer's letters; she holds Sévigné up as a model in all things, and she has a quotation ready for all occasions. Her love for the author of the letters is her most readily distinguishable characteristic, and indeed without it her character would hardly diverge from Proust's earlier models of self-abnegating maternal solicitude on the order of the mother in "La Confession d'une jeune fille." The grandmother's obsession with Sévigné marks her individually; along with her love of nature and of art, it sets her off as distinct from the mother. At the same time, her identification with Sévigné appears to be an identification with the idea of motherhood itself, making of her not only the grandmother but the Grand Mother.

After the grandmother's death, her daughter begins to resemble her more and more closely, seeming to take over her identity. One of the clearest elements of this transformation is the mother's fetishistic attachment to the grandmother's belongings, including "the volumes of Mme de Sévigné which my grandmother took with her everywhere, copies which my mother would not have exchanged even for the original manuscript of the *Letters*" (2:797; 3:167).

Sévigné's letters are doubly maternal in the novel: by virtue of both content and context they form the gospel of motherhood in the *Recherche*. The mother would not exchange the grandmother's copy of the letters for an original manuscript, because the volumes she has inherited have themselves become the original text.[4] The narrator makes a similar observation in *Le Temps retrouvé* about his own peculiar brand of bibliophilia: he would like to collect first editions, he says, but he stresses that by this he does not mean the first published editions of works. Instead, he would value those volumes which he himself had first read (3:922; 4:465). This form of fetishism operates on purely narcissistic rather than consumerist principles. The grandmother's edition of Sévigné has become the family Bible.

4. In fact the manuscript of the letters, as Proust may well have known, had been destroyed in the eighteenth century by order of Sévigné's granddaughter Pauline de Simiane. See my essay "The Law of the Mother: Proust and Mme de Sévigné," *Romanic Review* 85 (January 1994), 91–112.

What happens after the grandmother's death, then, appears to be that her daughter takes over her identity as desexualized mother, the Good Mother in the Kleinian sense.[5] Upon assuming the grandmother's cult of Sévigné, she no longer belongs to the father but is now entirely and selflessly devoted to her child. She becomes as free from the taint of sexuality as the "demoiselles Vinteuil" are eventually depicted as being in their sexless, selfless devotion to the memory of the late M. Vinteuil. As the latter case clearly demonstrates, though, idealization of the parent is inseparable from sexuality and from the drive to desecrate. This phenomenon occurs in much more subtly textualized form where the narrator's mother and grandmother are concerned. The depiction of the grandmother as desexualized mother—and therefore of the mother as desexualized by her identification with the grandmother—entails its own seamy underside, which manifests itself through references to Mme de Sévigné.

After the grandmother's death, the mother devotes herself not to her son but rather, with impressive single-mindedness, to the memory of her mother. She goes so far, the narrator notes in *Sodom et Gomorrhe*, as to express pleasure at the suffering he experiences as a result of the loss: "My own anguish . . . could not but make Mamma happy (notwithstanding all her affection for myself), like everything else that guaranteed my grandmother survival in people's hearts" (2:798; 3:167).

The mother's transformation into her own mother clearly entails not so much a reaffirmation of her maternal role as a cult of the mother-daughter bond, which finds its exemplary articulation in quotations from Sévigné. If the latter's writings form the consummate text of motherhood in the French canon, it is a very idiosyncratic maternal discourse that they offer, one to which oedipal models (according to which the

---

5. "The two types of object, good and bad, arise as a result of the splitting of the primary or original introjected object, i.e. the subject divides his conception of the breast, mother, father, penis, etc., into two, the good and bad breast, etc., thereby defending himself against the ambivalence which would ensue if he recognized that he experienced satisfaction and frustration from and love and hate towards the same object." Rycroft, *Critical Dictionary of Psychoanalysis*, 65. Although the concept of the Good Mother is most often associated with the work of Melanie Klein, as Rycroft notes, it had already been developed by Freud.

most perfect love is between mother and son) would not seem to apply.[6] Although she had a son, Sévigné's letters are love letters to her grown daughter, Mme de Grignan. They represent not just maternal devotion in general but a very ardent discourse of maternal devotion *to a daughter:* an exclusively female discourse, in short, of which the son can never figure as addressee.

Quotations from Sévigné's letters circulate in the novel between mother and daughter even after the grandmother's death, and they give voice to a hermetic female bond from which the narrator is necessarily excluded. For instance, in the passage in which the narrator's mother is seen assuming the grandmother's cult of Sévigné and taking comfort from his grief, the narrator goes on to remark that she has written him three letters before joining him in Balbec, and that, "in each of the three letters . . . she quoted Mme de Sévigné to me as though those three letters had been written not by her to me but by my grandmother to her" (2:797–98; 3:167).

Thus, even when the mother writes to her son, her quotations from Sévigné's letters are the sign of a primary relationship between mother and daughter of which he remains the observer. This passage neatly underscores the function of Sévigné's letters in the novel: the grandmother's attachment to Sévigné, which has previously appeared to indicate nothing more than her hyperbolic motherly accessibility (coupled with her penchant for filtering everything through "layers of art"), is now seen as the sign of the obstacle that blocks the narrator's access to the novel's maternal figures. They only have eyes—even, or especially, in death—for each other. While the grandmother is alive, she alone speaks the language of Sévigné's letters, but after her death, her absence elicits expressions of that same discourse from her daughter. It is not just that the mother must step into the now vacant place of the grandmother; that absence is in fact the catalyst of such discourse. Sévigné's passionate letters to her daughter owe their existence, after all, to Mme de Grignan's departure for Provence. Proust's narrator witnesses these epistolary expressions of mother-

<hr/>

6. "A mother is only brought unlimited satisfaction by her relation to a son; this is altogether the most perfect, the most free from ambivalence of all human relationships." Freud, "Femininity," 361.

daughter fidelity only because he becomes, in the grandmother's absence, their recipient by proxy.

The narrator's repeated insistence on the fact that the letters quoting Sévigné are three in number stresses what the statement suggests but never makes explicit: the triangulated relation among mother, grandmother, and narrator. Because of the mother's quotations of Sévigné, he recognizes that the letters he receives are not really addressed to him at all, but rather circulate inaccessibly between mother and daughter. Sévigné's name becomes the mark of a discourse that excludes him even as he reads it, much as Léa's references to Morel in the feminine demonstrate to Charlus that the letter he has opened "by mistake" speaks of a relation he cannot enter into or even understand.

The most important familial triangulation in the novel, I would argue, is not the oedipal scenario ostentatiously set up in "Combray" only to be knocked down by the father's abdication of the Abraham role and then his effective disappearance from the text, but rather this more unexpected Sévignesque triangle, of which two corners are female and which prepares the narrator for his subsequent obsession with sexual relations between women.

Leonardo with a Difference

In the final chapter of her *Male Subjectivity at the Margins,* Kaja Silverman proposes a reading of Proustian sexuality based on Freud's study of Leonardo da Vinci. Silverman identifies three distinct paradigms of male homosexuality in Freud's work. The first is the negative Oedipus complex, in which the subject identifies with his mother and desires his father (as opposed to the positive Oedipus complex, in which the little boy identifies with his father and desires his mother). The second is the Greek pederasty model, from which the mother is absent and which is predicated on narcissistic object choice: the subject identifies with the father and desires a version of himself as a youth. The third is the Leonardo da Vinci paradigm, which Silverman finds realized in Freud's study of Leonardo and in the *Recherche.* In the Leonardo paradigm, also predicated on narcissistic object choice, the father is absent; the subject identifies with his mother and desires a younger version of himself. What sets this model of sexuality apart from the other two, in Silverman's account, is not just that the cast of characters has changed slightly but that it is reversible. That is, not only does the subject identify with the mother and desire a version of his younger self whom he may love as his mother loved him, but also he is able to identify with his younger self and desire the mother.[7]

Silverman's use of the Leonardo paradigm to account for Proustian sexuality, it seems to me, accounts for the narrator's situation in all particulars but one. It is true that the father is absent, and also that an unusual reversibility characterizes the erotic configuration found in the *Recherche*. The narrator would like to identify alternately with the mother as desiring subject and with the object of her desire. As we have seen, reversibility is written into the account of maternal eroticism in the novel: once the grandmother has died, the mother takes over her role and writes to her son as though she were her own mother writing to herself.

The problem with Silverman's otherwise impeccable characterization of Proustian eroticism is that the object of maternal desire in the novel is always necessarily female. As Silverman amply demonstrates, the traditional oedipal triangle, in which the son identifies with his father and desires his mother, does not really obtain, however much it may appear to in the novel's opening pages. Oedipal desire is short-circuited in the *drame du coucher* or "goodnight kiss" passage because of the father's refusal to play his appointed role. The narrator himself recognizes that what he has depicted as paternal interdiction actually comes from the mother and grandmother: "Perhaps even what I called his severity, when he sent me off to bed, deserved that title less than my mother's or my grandmother's attitude" (1:40; 1:37).

Rather than displaying the standard positive oedipal situation that first seems to be his lot, then, as Silverman observes, the narrator both desires and identifies with the mother. The mother, too, situates desire and identification in a single object; that object, however, is not her husband, father, or son but her own mother. The narrator's triangulated configuration replicates the mother's own narcissistic object choice, except that

7. See Silverman, *Male Subjectivity at the Margins,* esp. 356–73.

there is no place in her scenario for him. Maternal desire circulates between mother and daughter, and the son is always somehow *de trop*, as becomes evident after the grandmother's death in the letters the mother writes to her son, in which she cites Sévigné's letters as the mark of maternal fidelity to a daughter.

Even in the *drame du coucher* scene the grandmother comes between mother and son: the books from which the mother proposes to read aloud are a present from the grandmother. The work chosen is *François le champi*. This choice of George Sand's novel, which reappears at the end of *Le Temps retrouvé* as part of the narrator's epiphanic series of involuntary memories, is a loaded one. The grandmother's great liking for Sand— which neither Proust himself nor the narrator (once past childhood) shares—at first seems simply to be a function of her love of nature, since the four books she gives her grandson are Sand's rustic novels.[8] It also, however, suggests an oblique nod in the direction of Gomorrah, given the novelist's much-discussed cross-dressing tendencies and apparent bisexuality.

The plot of *François le champi,* as numerous commentators have noted in connection with its appearance in this scene, concerns the growing love and eventual marriage between a woman and her adoptive son. It turns out that the selection of this particular Sand novel, with its almost farcically oedipal *mise-en-abyme* overtones in the context of the goodnight kiss scene, has to do with paternal decree. The father, we learn, has imposed his veto over the grandmother's choice of gift. He had found the grandmother's original choices (including *Indiana,* a more risqué work by Sand) unsuitable for an impressionable young mind, and she had modified her gift accordingly (1:39). The grandmother's thwarted desire to transmit her taste for George Sand (one of whose works, *Lélia,* involves an incestuous passion between sisters) suggests a buried Gomorrhean intertext even in the novel's most squarely oedipal passage.

The father's disappearance from the narrative does not eliminate triangulation, of course, nor does it betoken Silverman's configuration of mother, subject, and subject's former self. The narrator's implicit object of identification, as of desire, is the mother: the mother as alternatively

8. On Proust's attitude toward Sand, see 3:920; 4:463; see also 1:1118, n.2.

mother and daughter, his mother and his grandmother's daughter. He desires not his former self but his hypothetical self, the self he would have been if he had been born a daughter rather than a son. Thus, when Silverman asks the rhetorical question, "Why not think of Marcel simply as a lesbian?" the answer remains what common sense would dictate: because he is not a woman. As a son, he can find no place in a paradigm comprising only mothers and daughters.

The Grandmother between Sodom and Gomorrah

The narrator's obsessive desire to insert himself as object into Albertine's putatively lesbian psyche represents a reconfiguration of the grandmother-mother-son triangle and a symbolic attempt to penetrate the grandmother-mother couple. He insists, for instance, on aligning Albertine with the grandmother, imagining that he is responsible for both their deaths: "Juxtaposing the deaths of my grandmother and of Albertine, I felt that my life was defiled by a double murder from which only the cowardice of the world could absolve me" (3:506; 4:78). He has earlier, in "Combray," seen the imposition of his will on the mother—the other side of the *manque de volonté* coin—as prefiguring her death as well (1:41–42; 1:38). As the daughter's sexuality kills the mother in "La Confession d'une jeune fille," his desire itself will have killed all three: mother, grandmother, and girlfriend. In the *Recherche,* however, unlike in the early story, what is in question is not a passion that represents betrayal of the mother but rather the need to possess the maternal figure, whether in the form of the mother, the grandmother, or Albertine.

The parallelism between the grandmother and Albertine also resurfaces in the involuntary-memory phenomenon Proust refers to under the name of "the intermittences of the heart." This phrase, which serves as title for the section of *Sodome et Gomorrhe* in which the narrator belatedly gains full awareness of his grandmother's death, represented a concept of capital importance for Proust, who at one point had intended to use it as the title of the novel as a whole. It is generally understood as referring specifically to the peculiar amnesia-hypermnesia phenomenon the narrator experiences following his grandmother's death. The last section of

Sodome et Gomorrhe, though, in which Albertine reveals her tie to the "demoiselles Vinteuil," and thus, presumably, to Gomorrah, is called "Les Intermittences du coeur II." The volume as a whole is in fact structured around three a posteriori realizations, three items of knowledge of which, though all have long been obvious, the narrator becomes conscious only as the result of a traumatic revelation. In the courtyard, he suddenly understands that Charlus is really an invert; in his room at Balbec, that the grandmother is really dead; in the train, that Albertine is really a lesbian. The grandmother's death is thus framed by the narrator's discoveries of Sodom and Gomorrah. This juxtaposition of the exalted (grandmaternal purity) and the base (homosexual impurity) is underscored not only by the tripartite structure of these revelations and by the narrator's association of Albertine with the grandmother, but also by the grandmother's unerring appreciation of the novel's homosexual characters. She instinctively likes Mlle Vinteuil, Jupien, Saint-Loup, and Charlus, and her encomium always precedes the unveiling of each character's "true nature." In this way, although she is seen to have an excellent eye for what the narrator unfailingly misses in his dull-witted putative heterosexuality, she escapes implication in what her preferences reveal.

In *À l'ombre des jeunes filles en fleurs,* during the narrator's first trip to Balbec, he and his grandmother are introduced to Saint-Loup by Mme de Villeparisis and then to Charlus, uncle of the former and nephew of the latter. The narrator is disconcerted to recognize in Charlus the same penetrating gaze that had been fixed on him earlier in Balbec and earlier still in Combray, when the baron was generally assumed to be Mme Swann's illicit lover. The grandmother, by contrast, is enchanted by Charlus (2:812; 2:115). Her pleasure in his company is remarkable, since one of the first things we learn about her is her marked distaste for aristocratic distinctions. She nonetheless discerns in the eminently snooty Charlus a sensibility and an intelligence that allow her to ignore his evident class prejudice. What cements their bond is a common appreciation of Sévigné's letters.

Mme de Villeparisis, who knows of the grandmother's penchant for Sévigné but does not share it, asks her nephew Charlus to describe for her friend a château where the letter writer had stayed. He is thus presented both as an admirer of Sévigné's writing and as having access to privileged knowledge of her, a firsthand experience of her haunts. The discussion that ensues sets up an implicit contrast between Charlus and the grandmother, who understand Sévigné's love for her daughter, and Mme de Villeparisis, who emphatically does not. Mme de Villeparisis represents in this scene a normative point of view that cannot assimilate Sévigné's torrid discourse of maternal devotion into any received category and as a result dismisses it as insincere. She had already displayed her incomprehension of the sacred mother-daughter bond by expressing incredulity at the fact that the grandmother and mother exchange letters daily ("What, your daughter writes to you *every day*? But what on earth can you find to say to each other?" [1:749; 2:56]). Her immunity to Sévigné's charm seems to stem from her being an aunt rather than a mother. While Charlus is, of course, no more a mother than is Mme de Villeparisis, his comprehension of Sévigné evidently has to do with his being a *tante:* it is his inversion that allows him to appreciate what is at stake in her letters.[9]

When Mme de Villeparisis remarks dismissively that Sévigné's attachment to "that tiresome Mme de Grignan" smacks of "literature"—that is, artifice—Charlus responds with a vigorous defense that hinges on a tacit interpretation of her letters to her daughter as love letters. In the seventeenth century, he says, "feelings of that sort were thoroughly understood" (1:818; 2:121), and cites as evidence two La Fontaine fables, "The

---

9. Mme de Villeparisis would seem to provide a peculiar exception to Richard Goodkin's compelling argument about "avuncularity" and homosexuality in *Around Proust,* since she is at once eminently auntly and relentlessly uncomprehending of alternative conceptions of love. Although he states in a note that his use of the term "avuncularity" is not meant to be gender-specific (148, n.3), his analysis is almost exclusively concerned with male characters. Goodkin maintains that "Charlus is the most 'avuncular' character in the novel, being both Saint-Loup's uncle and Mme de Villeparisis's nephew" (149, n.19). I would, perhaps too literal-mindedly, disagree with him on this point. Charlus is the most avuncular character only in the figurative sense of Goodkin's argument, that is, because of the link he wishes to establish between avuncularity and homosexuality in the novel. For instance, the duc de Guermantes, a singularly un-avuncular character in Goodkin's terms, shares Charlus's familial status by virtue of being his brother. Instead of Charlus, therefore, I would maintain that it is Mme de Villeparisis who most clearly incarnates at least a literal "avuncularity," having been raised by an aunt, and being the aunt of all the Guermantes and the sister of a famous aunt (Mme de Beausergent, author of *Mémoires d'une tante*).

Two Friends" and "The Two Pigeons," both of which are about male friendship, and both suffused with homoeroticism. Although the obstinately clueless narrator makes nothing of this at the time, the alert rereader cannot escape seeing in this speech a foreshadowing of what we later learn about Charlus.

The scene could not take place in full textual consciousness of the baron's "true nature." If Charlus had been overtly presented as a Sodomite at this juncture, his defense of Sévigné would necessarily suppose a reading of her love for her daughter as incestuous lesbian passion, thus implicating both Sévigné and the grandmother in his understanding of what he calls "feelings of that sort." As it is, with the revelation of what prompts Charlus's interest in seventeenth-century literature still several volumes off, the grandmother can concur wholeheartedly in his interpretation of the letters. She is pleased to find a kindred soul. The narrator reports: "My grandmother was delighted to hear the Letters thus spoken of, exactly as she would have spoken of them herself. She was astonished that a man could understand them so well. She found in M. de Charlus a delicacy, a sensibility that were quite feminine" (1:818–19; 2:121).

The tie between Charlus and the grandmother, unlikely textual bedfellows though they may be, is underscored by several factors. Charlus himself at one point exploits their common interest in Sévigné in such a way that both the letter writer and the grandmother are posthumously conscripted into the service of his too keen interest in the narrator. In *Guermantes II*, as part of his failed attempt to seduce the benighted young man, he has a "curious edition" of Sévigné bound specially for his friend, in memory of the latter's grandmother (2:585; 2:851).[10]

Perhaps most strikingly, though, the baron, whose first name is Palamède, is known in the intimate circle of his family and friends as "Mémé." *Mémé* is the familiar name by which bourgeois French children traditionally call their grandmothers. Proust's narrator would seem to be an exception to this practice, which is what allows Charlus's nickname to

---

10. Moncrief and Kilmartin translate "curieuse édition" as "rare edition," which is to my mind unfortunate because of the prurient undertones of the adjective *curieuse*.

pass without comment in the book. Lest this detail be dismissed as an insignificant aristocratic quirk—as indeed the narrator seems to do—it should be noted that "Mémé" is hardly the most phonetically obvious diminutive of Palamède, which would seem to lend itself more readily, for instance, to "Papa." But Charlus is not, for all his mentoring, a paternal figure; again, he is above all a *vieille tante.*

According to the proleptic logic of the narrative, once arrived at *Sodome et Gomorrhe,* we are retrospectively to see in Charlus's understanding of Sévigné a sign of his essentially feminine nature, and thus of his vice. Because the grandmother is not presented as subject to the binary logic of paradox which governs the double nature of the invert, Proust never invites us to re-read this scene in terms of what it reveals about the grandmother herself. Such a re-reading would necessarily call into question the purity of maternal love as textualized in Sévigné's letters, suggesting that the grandmother also sees the letter writer's passion for her daughter as an example of same-sex love rather than simply the most canonically privileged example of maternal devotion. Further remarks by Charlus in this same conversation, moreover, reinforce the homoerotic reading of Sévigné. The narrator seems to be baiting the reader with premature clues to Charlus's true nature, dangling irresistible evidence of his vice before us and then hiding it behind the veil of grandmaternal purity. If the grandmother likes the baron, he seems to suggest, Charlus cannot be the pervert we may suspect him of being. Since we later discover that he is, however, this discovery must call into question grandmaternal purity itself.

Mme de Villeparisis, still skeptical about the sincerity of Sévigné's professions of love for Mme de Grignan, intervenes in the discussion, reminding her nephew that "it wasn't 'love' in her case, since it was her daughter." To this dampeningly normative remark Charlus replies that her definition of love is insufficient: " 'But what matters in life is not whom or what one loves,' he went on, in a judicial, peremptory, almost cutting tone, 'it is the fact of loving.' " Its cryptic nature underscored by the string of modifiers that interrupts it, this pronouncement is a proleptically unmistakable allusion to what we later learn about Charlus's nature. He continues his attack on narrowly conceived definitions of love with more references to seventeenth-century literature and, finally, uses Sévigné's son to illustrate his point about the unworthiness of heterosexuality to figure as the defining mode of passion: "What Mme de Sévigné felt for her daughter has a far better claim to rank with the passion that Racine described in *Andromaque* or *Phèdre* than the commonplace relations young Sévigné had with his mistresses" (1:819; 2:122).

The argument Charlus advances here is a complicated one. The primary contrast he sets up is between "real passion" as exemplified in Sévigné's letters to her daughter and the banal heterosexual dalliances of her son Charles. The ultimate measure of passion he invokes, though, still within the context of seventeenth-century French literature, is that of Racinian tragedy, and the specific plays to which he refers showcase maternal devotion. He thereby stacks the deck, as it were, since in the context of these plays motherhood is already valorized as the primary mode of passion. Both *Andromaque* and *Phèdre* are centrally about mothers and sons: the former concerns the Trojan widow's attempts to fend off a suitor and save her son, while the latter features the eponymous heroine's quasi-incestuous passion for her stepson. According to Charlus's analogy, Sévigné's love for Mme de Grignan must be read as at once as disturbing, all-encompassing, and clearly erotic as Phèdre's for Hippolyte, and as innocent, "truly" maternal, and pure as Andromaque's for Astyanax. Thus we find the two faces of the grandmother-mother relation in the novel as read through Sévigné: simultaneously the privileged incarnation of all that is most untouchably pure in the novel and, by implication, an incestuous precursor of Gomorrah.

Charles de Sévigné

"Young Sévigné," who figures in Charlus's argument as the representative of vapid heterosexuality as opposed to the "real" passion of his mother for her daughter, merits scrutiny in this context. Mme de Grignan's hapless brother appears in his mother's letters as the subject of many humorous anecdotes, often involving his ill-starred amorous adventures—so much so that Mme de Sévigné herself might have concurred in Charlus's portrayal of their respective emotional lives. He is also repeatedly invoked by the mother in the *Recherche,* who at several junctures compares the narrator to Sévigné's charming but dissolute son.

The crux of the comparison is always, significantly, what Proust calls *manque de volonté:* Charles de Sévigné could not make up his mind. He is portrayed in his mother's letters as being "of distressing weakness; he is at everyone's disposal."[11] He drifts from one momentarily passionate affair to another, in her depiction, unable to figure out what to do with himself, and spending money pointlessly all the while. His mother serves up his social, financial, and sexual misadventures for the amusement of Mme de Grignan. Sévigné describes in some detail, for instance, an unfortunate interlude in 1671 in which Charles became involved simultaneously with the famed courtesan Ninon de Lenclos, who not only was old enough to be his mother (in fact, she was older than his mother), but also had twenty years earlier been his father's mistress; and with La Champmeslé, the young actress who later originated the role of Phèdre. Ninon unceremoniously dumped Charles after a month-long liaison in which she described him, his mother repeats with rueful pleasure, as "the merest watergruel creature! . . . a body of wet paper, a heart as cold as pumpkin fried in snow."[12] Following his breakup with Ninon, Charles found himself unable to perform sexually with La Champmeslé, a bout of impotence that he not only recounted to his mother but blamed on her as well: "He told me he fancied I had given him some of my ice, that he did not desire to resemble me in that particular, and that I had better have conferred it on my daughter."[13]

Sévigné seems amused by this interpretation, and of course immediately relates it to the daughter who should, according to Charles, have inherited their mother's supposed frigidity. Charles's presumably jocular

11. "Il est d'une faiblesse à faire mal au coeur; il est tout ce qu'il plaît aux autres." Letter of April 22, 1671, in *Letters from the Marchioness de Sévigné,* 7 vols. (London: Spurr & Swift, 1927), 1:122; Mme de Sévigné, *Correspondance,* 3 vols., ed. Roger Duchêne (Paris: Gallimard, 1972–78), 1:227. Subsequent references will be to these two editions, with date of letter and volume and page numbers. Translations have been altered in places for diction and accuracy.

12. "Une âme de bouillie . . . un corps de papier mouillé, un coeur de citrouille fricassé dans de la neige." April 22, 1671, 1:123; 1:228; see also April 8, 1671, 1:106; 1:210.

13. April 8, 1671, 1:105–6; 1:211.

accusation neatly combines hostility and identification. Like Proust's narrator, he associates his inability to perform with his mother while acting it out in terms of a maternal substitute (Albertine, in the latter case). Charles seems to be complaining that his resemblance to his mother is what prevents him from assuming his father's role; if he were less like his mother, he might be able to have her, both in the form of Ninon and by deposing his sister.[14] The latter, having escaped this icy inheritance, has become the central object of maternal desire; his mother is "frigid" only with him. Charles's seductive and resentful confessions are quickly recycled as offerings in the mother-daughter commerce of seduction and complicity.

In the *Recherche,* as we have seen in Charlus's defense of nontraditional forms of love, Charles de Sévigné is held up as an example of heterosexual unworthiness. The narrator's mother too, cites him in warnings to her son about his financial profligacy, and also in her expressions of disapproval of his relationship with Albertine, whom she aligns with Sévigné's unappreciative depictions of various potential daughters-in-law. In one instance in *La Prisonnière,* the narrator receives a letter from his mother that indirectly, through references to Sévigné, suggests her unhappiness with Albertine. One of her citations is particularly revealing:

Without referring to what distressed her most, she expressed displeasure at my lavish expenditure: "Where on earth does all your money go? It is distressing enough that, like Charles de Sévigné, you do not know what you want and are 'two or three people at once,' but do try at least not to be like him in spending money so that I may never have to say of you: He has discovered how to spend and have nothing to show, how to lose without staking and how to pay without clearing himself of debt." (3:137; 3:647)

The portrait of Charles that emerges from this quotation is indeed unflattering, not merely that of a ne'er-do-well but of a ridiculous incompetent. Proust, whose financial speculations consumed a good deal of

14. Henri de Sévigné was long dead by this point; he was killed in a duel over another woman when both children were small.

his attention and fortune after his parents' death, was sufficiently fond of this characterization of the financially dissolute Charles to apply the same formula to himself, comparing himself to Sévigné's son more than once in his own correspondence.[15] As the passage itself suggests, though, the narrator's pecuniary misadventures are not the central focus of his mother's discontent. Her references to Charles de Sévigné's financial profligacy mask her more pressing worries about her son: that he is wasting his time with Albertine, as Charles did with his various dalliances, and more generally that, again like Charles, he does not know what he wants. Charles de Sévigné becomes the poster boy for *manque de volonté* in the novel, as his mother is the patron saint of motherhood.

When the narrator's mother laments his inability to decide on a course of action by comparing him to Sévigné's portrait of her son, she couches her objection in general terms and then cites a specific moment from one of Sévigné's letters: like Charles, the narrator is "two or three people at the same time." The phrase to which she refers appears in a letter to Mme de Grignan in which Sévigné relates a remarkable letter she has had from Charles:

> My son sends me strange ravings: he tells me that there is a certain "he" who adores me, and another "he" who is the torment of my life, and that the two had a serious encounter the other day at les Rochers. I wrote him back that I wished the one had killed the other, so that I might no longer have three children, that the last of them was the cause of all my maternal woes, and that if he could strangle him himself, I would be only too happy with the two others.[16]

The idea of Charles as "two or three people at once," then, taken in its original context, does not merely refer to indecisiveness, but also establishes the link between *manque de volonté* and maternal profanation.

---

15. See, e.g., Proust, *Correspondance,* 14:199, 15:333. As Ghislain de Diesbach, who recounts Proust's misadventures on the stock market in his biography, remarks, this characterization by Sévigné of her son becomes "the leitmotif of his correspondence," especially during the war. Diesbach, *Proust,* 588.

16. November 2, 1679, 6:156–57; 2:727.

Charles contains within himself warring factions that represent, respectively, filial devotion and matricidal rage, like Henri van Blarenberghe in "Sentiments filiaux d'un parricide." This essay, which Proust wrote in 1907 about a notorious case of matricide-suicide (the French term *parricide* doing duty for both matricide and patricide), whose perpetrator had been an acquaintence of his, juxtaposes van Blarenberghe's vicious murder of his mother with the tender filial piety he had earlier expressed in a letter of condolence written to the author at the death of Mme Proust. (One of the most provocative details in this story, it should be added, is that the newspaper *Le Matin* had erroneously identified the police commissioner who came upon van Blarenberghe just before the latter succumbed to his self-inflicted gunshot wound as "M. Proust." Thus life, or at least journalism, imitated Proust's early fiction.)[17]

The mother's reference to Charles de Sévigné's being "two or three people at once" implicates the narrator, certainly, in the necessarily double nature of filial devotion exemplified by Henri van Blarenberghe and also by the "sadism" of Mlle Vinteuil in the Montjouvain scene. What is particularly revealing about this citation, though, is that the passage from Sévigné's original letter also suggests the complement of parental desecration, which is left entirely unexplored in the *Recherche:* maternal rage, the mother's desire to kill the problematic son, or at least the problematic version of the son. In "Sentiments filiaux d'un parricide," Proust cites Mme van Blarenberghe's reported last words to her son: "What have you done to me! What have you done to me!" He then ruminates on their universal applicability:

> If we let ourselves think for a few moments we shall, I believe, agree that there is probably no devoted mother who could not, when her last day dawns, address the same reproach to her son. The truth is that, as we

---

17. Proust's article as it originally appeared in *Le Figaro* contained a mention of this remarkable coincidence, although it is relegated to an endnote by the editors of the Pléiade volume in which it is reproduced. See Marcel Proust, *Contre Sainte-Beuve,* ed. Pierre Clarac and Yves Sandre (Paris: Gallimard, 1971), 157, n.3, and 785. The translation "Filial Sentiments of a Parricide," appears in *Pleasures and Days;* subsequent references will be to the translation and the Pléiade text consecutively.

grow older, we kill what loves us by reason of the cares we lay on it, by reason of that uneasy tenderness that we inspire and keep forever stretched upon the rack. (304; 158–59; translation modified)

This Wildean idea that "each man kills the thing he loves"—which becomes, in Proust's terms, the thing that loves him—is put forth as a general law in Proust's writings, but it is seen, at least explicitly, as going only one way. The child kills the parent; parental desecration is the flip side of filial devotion. The reference to Sévigné's letter about Charles's double nature opens the question that Proust does not deal with directly, since he is always exploring filial guilt and never approaches the mother-son relation from the point of view of the mother. That task is left to Sévigné herself. If, as Proust insists in the essay on van Blarenberghe, the idea that "we kill what loves us" expresses the human condition, then the mother is no more exempt than the son. If the narrator's mother in the novel is displeased by the evidence that her son is, like Charles de Sévigné, "two or three people at once," then she too harbors a desire to kill at least one of those selves. The Sévigné intertext makes clear what the novel itself relentlessly glosses over: that mother and son are locked in a murderous battle of wills that is fought under the guilt- and resentment-filled auspices of *manque de volonté,* and in which the stakes involve the narrator's sexuality as well as his artistic vocation.

The Non-oedipal Triangle

The novel's references to Charles de Sévigné serve to explain what remains otherwise inexplicable: the narrator's obsessive interest in women who prefer other women. His lesbophilia, as it might be termed, cannot be based on a familial configuration that is either positively or negatively oedipal, since the oedipal triangle set up in "Combray" quickly disappears along with the father. Nor does it embody what Silverman identifies as a "Leonardo model," grounded in reversible identification with and desire for a mother figure whose primary object is her son. Desire is indeed triangulated in the novel, but what is in question is an entirely different triangle consisting of the narrator, his mother, and his grandmother. The couple formed by the mother and grandmother is articulated primarily through a discourse borrowed from Sévigné's letters to her daughter, in which the son figures only as an object of epistolary exchange between mother and daughter. The narrator's attempts to read himself into these exclusively female relations leave him in the position of receiving letters expressing a maternal desire that is ultimately not addressed to him.

What happens when Proust divides the maternal function between mother and grandmother in the *Recherche* is that the passionate, hermetic relation between the two prefigures the explicitly erotic relations between women which the narrator presents under the name Gomorrah. I have argued that the grandmother, in all her pristine purity as asexual mother figure, is linked to the "cities of the plain" through Sévigné's letters, and most clearly through Charlus's reading of Sévigné. In fact, this other face of the grandmother is present by implication from the very beginning of the novel. Immediately before the first mention of the grandmother in the opening pages of "Combray," the narrator depicts the magic lantern slide show that transforms his room into an allegorical chamber. The picture he describes illustrates the medieval legend of Golo and Geneviève de Brabant, as the lubricious would-be ravisher advances toward the château of the innocent lady: "Riding at a jerky trot [*au pas saccadé de son cheval*], Golo, filled with an infamous design, issued from the little triangular forest which dyed dark green the slope of a convenient hill, and advanced fitfully towards the castle of poor Geneviève de Brabant" (1:10; 1:9). The nature of Golo's "infamous design" is highlighted by the sexual overtones of the landscape through which he rides, with its triangular forest shading the slope of a hill. Golo's approach itself announces his complicity with the female body. The narrator's commentary on this image reinforces the oedipal reading that these pages seem to demand, as it increases his desire to "fall into the arms of my mother, whom the misfortunes of Geneviève de Brabant had made all the dearer to me, just as the crimes of Golo had driven me to a more than ordinarily scrupulous examination of my own conscience" (1:11; 1:10).

All is thus as it should be: the narrator in his guilty oedipal desire plays Golo to his mother's blameless Geneviève de Brabant (who, according to the legend, repels the concupiscent traitor despite her husband's absence). One detail in his description of Golo, however, alerts us that this classic oedipal moment is not exactly as it appears to be. Golo is twice portrayed through the use of the expression "pas saccadé," in the passage quoted earlier ("au pas saccadé de son cheval, Golo . . .") and again later in the same paragraph: "then he rode away at the same jerky trot" ("puis il s'éloignait du même pas saccadé" (1.11; 1.10). On the very next page we meet the grandmother for the first time: she is walking in the garden, despite the bad weather, with "her keen, jerky little step" ("de son petit pas enthousiaste et saccadé" [1:12; 1:11]).

The jerky gait that, in the case of Golo, expresses both the imperfect technology of the magic lantern and the character's menacing sexuality is thus reproduced in the grandmother's innocent, nature-loving stroll in the garden during a storm. The father, like Geneviève de Brabant's husband, is entirely absent from this scenario, but what the repetition of the phrase "pas saccadé" suggests is that, despite the narrator's identification with Golo's designs on the lady, someone else has got there first. The grandmother, not the father, is the narrator's rival for his mother's affections.

The narrator's subsequent quest to penetrate the mystery of erotic relations between women has its origin in this familial triangle involving the mother, the grandmother, and the son who would be a daughter. One of the most salient characteristics of Gomorrah is the evident narcissism of relations between women: each desires her like, and they all resemble one another. When he first encounters the "petite bande" of "jeunes filles en fleurs," the narrator cannot settle on a single object of desire because they are indistinguishable to him. What he really desires is their interdependence on one another, as well as their independence from him: like the mother and grandmother, they form a seamless whole. Thus Proust's narrator desires women who desire other women not despite the fact but precisely because they evidently do not need him. It is in imitation of this resemblance between subject and object that the project of *recherche* finally comes to fruition: turning away from the doomed attempt to insert himself between women, the narrator decides to reproduce himself.

Conclusion

Proust, Marcel, and Gender Theory

Among the many traps Proust sets for the reader of *À la recherche du temps perdu,* surely the stickiest and most unavoidable is the question of biographical referentiality. The novel is and is not autobiographical; the narrator necessarily both is and is not the author. No force of theoretical sophistry can entirely bypass this conundrum. Proust was unable to resist flaunting it in the hapless reader's face: after thousands of pages of namelessness, in *La Prisonnière* his narrator posits a hypothetical condition in which he might share the first name of the author (3:69; 3:583; see also 3:154; 3:663). This spasm of autobiographical bet-hedging has encouraged generations of readers and critics to call Marcel a character who in fact remains carefully unnamed.

The problem is so basic and so inescapable as to have become invisible. Still, it remains a problem, so that, for instance, when Silverman asks, "Why not think of Marcel simply as a lesbian?" the inherent difficulties in carrying out the exhortation do not stop at "simply" and "lesbian" but extend to "Marcel" as well.

Critics often refer to the protagonist or the narrator, or both, as Marcel partly because of the passage in *La Prisonnière* in which he says that this might be construed as his name, and also because from the start he implicitly invites us to, by saying "I" frequently while declining to assign himself an alternative name. Furthermore, in doing so he is playing to—

and with—a deep readerly need to name, and to read biographically. It is awkward, as I have had ample occasion to observe, to deprive oneself of the ability to name. If I have resisted the impulse to call Proust's narrator Marcel, however, it is not only because I was schooled at a time when the death of the author had already been announced and postmortems were well under way. It is also because I believe that this issue, although it may seem entirely irrelevant to the discussion of Proust's depiction of lesbianism which forms the basis of this study, actually goes to the heart of the matter.

Proust baits the reader both by refusing definitively to name his narrator and, even more basically, by positing a narrator who so strongly resembles the author. Even the points of divergence, as critics have long observed, suggest, by denial, resemblance. Thus Proust, a half-Jewish homosexual, creates a gentile heterosexual narrator who displays a remarkably keen interest in Judaism and homosexuality, and in convergences between the two.

Proust's remark to Gide that "one may say anything as long as one does not say 'I' " seems on the whole both to account for his modus operandi, especially in matters sexual, and to have failed as a strategy of self-concealment. He appears to have given himself free rein to explore his most unseemly obsessions, taking care to attribute them to characters other than his protagonist. The fact that this gambit has never prevented readers from translating rigorously third-person pronouncements "back" into the "original" first person is itself depicted *en abyme* in the novel, in its merciless portrayal of what Eve Sedgwick calls "the glass closet." The *Recherche* contains numerous examples of this phenomenon, in the form of characters who present an entertainingly transparent spectacle as a result of the erroneous belief that they can showcase their most embarrassing secrets with impunity, provided they do so by denial and under cover of the third person (e.g., Charlus and homosexuality, Legrandin and snobbery).

Only a handful of factors provide essential distinctions between Proust and his protagonist. The most immediately obvious (I am leaving aside the fact that the narrator is surrounded by people who bear different names from those of the people Proust knew) is their respective familial configurations. The narrator is an only child, and in this he fulfills the murderous wish directed at siblings which psychoanalytic literature has so amply explored. According to Freudian theory, the impulse to be rid of a sibling, like oedipal rage against the father, betokens a desire to gain exclusive access to the mother. In Proust's novel, as we have seen, even in the absence of the brother, the ostensibly classic oedipal triangle of son, mother, and father is replaced by an idiosyncratic variant consisting of son, mother, and grandmother.

A second great difference between author and narrator is technical: Proust was busy writing the *Recherche* at the same time that his protagonist finds himself in the grip of what is surely the most fully documented case of writer's block in literary history. It is only at the end of this lengthy narrative of a failed literary vocation that the protagonist decides it is time to set aside worldly considerations and take up the pen for good.

The third major difference lies in the novel's erotic configurations. By this I do not mean that Proust was homosexual whereas his narrator is ostensibly, even ostentatiously, heterosexual. Rather, the salient distinction is that both are fascinated by male homosexuality, but the latter's consuming obsession with lesbianism, alone among his central preoccupations, has no apparent counterpart in the life of the author. Nothing in Proust's letters or the testimony of those who knew him suggests much of an interest in lesbians or lesbianism. It is surely this difference, combined with the common wisdom which dictates that among men, only heterosexuals find lesbianism compelling (homosexuals, according to this theory, operate on an exclusively phallic principle), which has led critics to see Gomorrah as a screen for something else.

What I would suggest instead is that Gomorrah be read as the signpost of fictionality in the *Recherche*. It is his lesbophilia that sets Proust's narrator apart from the author, that marks the novel as a novel rather than a perverse exercise in selective autobiography.

Proust's Gomorrah belongs, as I have suggested, to the fictional tradition that stretches roughly from *Mademoiselle de Maupin* and *La Fille aux yeux d'or* (both published in 1835) to *Goldfinger* and beyond. And yet Albertine is not precisely an avatar of Balzac's Paquita, nor is she Pussy Galore *avant la lettre*. According to this convention, allegedly designed by and for a male heterosexual mentality, the women's equivocal sexuality presents a challenge that can always, at least in principle, be met. Pussy Galore is depicted as impenetrable, only to be penetrated by the irresistibly phallic James Bond. Even Bilitis ends up a prosperous courtesan. Albertine, however, remains a sexual fugitive.

This distinction has everything to do with the remarkably non-phallocentric sexual economy of the *Recherche,* in which penetration is a purely epistemological category, and Gomorrah is throughout the novel figured as impenetrable. The narrator is most disturbed by Albertine's lesbian desires because he knows that he could never satisfy them, for, somehow, he does not have what it takes. The notion of male inadequacy that this implies is to a certain extent in accordance with time-honored depictions of female sexual insatiability (as in Baudelaire's "Sed non satiata," the title of which is taken from the Latin poet Juvenal).

Proust's representation of female sexuality diverges from this tradition, however, in that the latter is based on an idea of female rapacity and phallic inadequacy, of woman as a bottomless hole that no extant male equipment can fill: whence Lacan's Platonic ideal of "the phallus." The *Recherche* posits instead a sexual economy that is not based on a phallic standard. In Lacanian terms, it would seem that in Proust, only lesbians have "the phallus," except that Lacanian terms do not apply, because the phallus is nowhere at issue, any more than is the penis. The cultural tradition in which Lacanian theory operates, in fact, contains no terms with which to account for a model of sexuality such as that which Gomorrah represents, one that radically departs from a phallic economy.

This alternative way of imagining sexual politics is precisely what lesbian-feminist gender theory has tried to propose. It has not looked to authors such as Proust because of the unlikelihood that a male author, a paragon of gay male modernism, would provide a model for rethinking difference and sameness in terms of female eroticism. Proust himself clearly, if not unambivalently, wished to pave the way for a more tolerant acceptance of a specific mode of sexual difference. Perhaps in spite of himself—or perhaps not—he may now belatedly lend his efforts to the search for a new way of thinking about sexualities in general.

Index